For Meghan, Feb. 2021
From your friend,

John van der Stelt

a.k.a. Hammerson Peters

MYSTERIES OF CANADA

VOLUME II

© 2020 Mysteries of Canada

Publisher's Website:

www.MysteriesOfCanada.com

© 2020 Hammerson Peters

Author's Website:

www.HammersonPeters.com

Edited by Winston Kinnaird

Books by the same author:

Legends of the Nahanni Valley (2018)

Mysteries of Canada: Volume I (2019)

The Oak Island Encyclopedia (2019)

Mysteries of Canada

Volume II

By
Hammerson Peters

TABLE OF CONTENTS

Map of Canada..8

Acknowledgements..10

Introduction..12

Necromancy..14

    The Mystery of the Shaking Tent........................15

    The Ouija Board of Cobden, Ontario..................51

Cryptozoology..57

    Harrison Hot Springs: The Sasquatch
    Capital of Canada..58

    The Giant River Snake of
    Southeast Alberta..67

    Giant White Wolf Spotted in
    Northern Saskatchewan..79

    Traverspine Gorilla: A Wildman
    from Labrador..84

    Crawler Sighting in the
    Northwest Territories..89

    Kelly Chamandy: Canada's
    Last Bear Oil Salesman......................................120

Mad Scientists...131
    Granger Taylor: The Spaceman of
    Vancouver Island..132
    Tom Sukanen: The Crazy Finn
    of Saskatchewan..143
    The Tragedies of Gilbert Hedden
    and Welsford Parker..................................157

Ghosts of the Grand Railway Hotels...............184
    Ghostly Tales of the
    Banff Springs Hotel....................................185
    Ghostly Tales of the
    Prince of Wales Hotel................................190

The Unknown...196
    Canada's Lost Worlds................................197
    Top 5 Canadian Conspiracy Theories......216
    The Legend of Old Wives Lake................227
    The Phenomenon of Lost Time in Canada...............230

Miracles and Mirages....................................235
    The Miracle at Loon Lake........................236
    The Phantom Train of Medicine Hat........253
    Nautical Mysteries of Canada's Great Lakes...........259

Note from the Author..................................286
Bibliography...287

Mysteries of Canada: Volume II

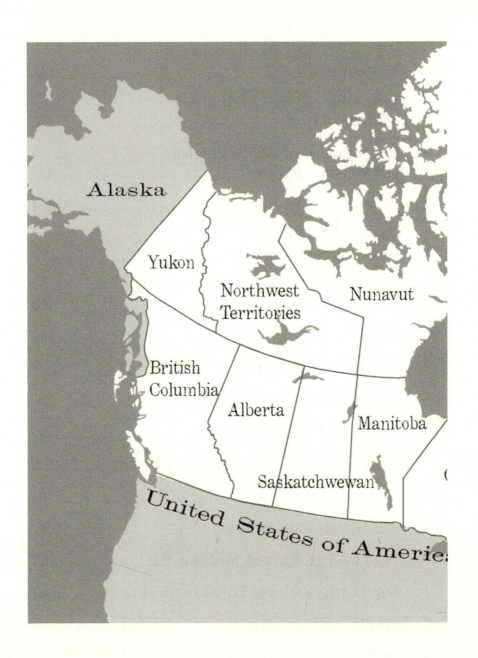

Map of Canada

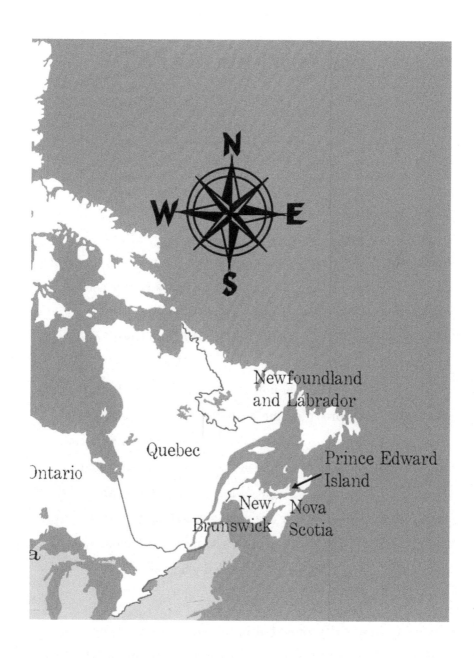

ACKNOWLEDGEMENTS

READERS OF MY BOOKS *'Legends of the Nahanni Valley'*, *'The Oak Island Encyclopedia'*, and *'Mysteries of Canada: Volume I'* may have noticed a particular name which consistently appears in my books' 'Acknowledgements' sections- that of Mr. Gary S. Mangiacopra. Gary is among the most diligent and eminent Fortean archivists in North America, 'Fortean' being the study of unexplained phenomena. Over the past four years, he has generously provided me with countless forgotten newspaper and magazine articles from his personal files, without which none of my books could have been written. *Mysteries of Canada: Volume II* is no exception to this pattern; many stories in this book are either based on or inspired by material from Mr. Mangiacopra's archive, and as always, I am deeply grateful for his continued assistance and friendship.

I am equally indebted to my editor, Mr. Winston Kinnaird, for his tremendous generosity, his impeccable command of the English language, and his incredible ability

Acknowledgements

to pick out grammatical, punctuation, and even spelling mistakes in material which has been reviewed time and time again by yours truly. No matter how many times I pore over my work in an attempt to iron out the wrinkles, checking and re-checking for errors, Winston, after going through my final drafts, somehow manages to produce an embarrassingly-long list of corrections, the rectification of which has a wonderful effect on the readability of my prose. As always, I cannot thank him enough for his essential services.

I would be remiss if I neglected to thank the following ladies and gentlemen for supplying this author with, and permitting him to publish, their personal anecdotes, which elevate this book from an accumulation of purely historical tales to more comprehensive collection of Forteana relevant to the modern reader: Justin Watkins, Don Herbert, Missy Sterling, Monty Chamandy, Ray Pulkanen, Carlene Graham, Patrick, L.B., Julie of Cardiff, Bella, Dell Marie Lamb, Ray Bosch, and Brian Gale.

Special thanks is due to DemonGirl99 and Cryptidical for allowing me to publish samples of their excellent artwork in this book.

Last, but certainly not least, from the bottom of my heart, I would like to thank my readers for their patronage, loyalty, and encouragement. This book is for you.

INTRODUCTION

THIS BOOK IS the second volume of the 'Mysteries of Canada' series, the first issue of which I published in 2019. Most of the stories contained herein were initially published in article format on the website MysteriesOfCanada.com throughout the year 2019, while a few constitute older articles which I published on my own website, HammersonPeters.com, from 2014 to 2016. Some of the stories are of a historical nature, others are completely modern, and all contain some element of the mysterious, the supernatural, or the unexplained.

I have divided this book into six thematic categories:

In **Necromancy**, we'll look at tales of divination, in which two very different types of conjurors attempted to acquire hidden knowledge through the use of occult apparatuses believed by some to facilitate communication with the spirits of the dead.

In **Cryptozoology**, we'll explore Canadian 'cryptid' stories- tales of strange animals said to haunt Canada's rivers,

Introduction

forests, mountains, and skies- from obscure First Nations legends to historic Sasquatch encounters to modern day monster sightings.

In **Mad Scientists,** we'll learn the stories of three eccentric engineers from across the country, from Welsford Parker, who tried his hand at solving the 200-year-old mystery of Oak Island, Nova Scotia, using a strange invention based on mysterious new technology, to Vancouver Island's Granger Taylor, who told his friends that he'd be abducted by aliens... before vanishing without a trace.

In **Ghosts of the Grand Railway Hotels,** we'll take a look at some of the spectral guests said to walk the halls of the Banff Springs Hotel in Banff National Park, and the Prince of Wales Hotel in Waterton Provincial Park- enchanting, storied chateaus nestled in the heart of the Albertan Rockies.

In **The Unknown,** we'll dive into Canadian conspiracy theories, travellers' tales of lost worlds, UFO sightings, and an old Indian ghost story.

Finally, in **Miracles and Mirages,** we'll look at stories of mysterious apparitions, from a forgotten tale of the Canadian prairies to sailors' yarns about the ghostly fleet said to sail the Great Lakes.

Enjoy!

NECROMANCY

THE MYSTERY OF THE SHAKING TENT

IN 1920, AN ENGLISH adventurer named Michael H. Mason explored much of Northern Canada by dogsled. Four years later, he published an account of his experience in a book entitled *The Arctic Forests*.

Mason's book is formatted like an encyclopedia, outlining the natural history of Northern Canada and the ethnology of its human inhabitants. On the subject of the spiritual beliefs of the Gwich'in Indians he encountered during his travels, Mason wrote:

"It is no easy task to write on the habits and philosophy of these most interesting and attractive people, for their most outstanding characteristic is general inconsistency."

Mason's observation could be applied more broadly to the spiritual beliefs held by all Canadian First Nations prior to their introduction to Christianity. There are about as many native Canadian religions as there are First Nations, each with its own collection of deities, legends, rituals, and superstitions. The Blackfoot of the western prairies, for example, had their Sun Dances- brutal ceremonies revolving around pain, sacrifice, and physical endurance. The Ojibwa of the Great Lakes had nuanced beliefs regarding the consumption of human flesh, considering the practice justifiable in times of war and horribly dangerous in times of famine. And the Haida of the Queen Charlotte Islands had their carved cedar masks representing the various spiritual entities that populate their mythology, wearing them in their dances and shamanic ceremonies.

In spite of their fundamental differences, many of Canada's pre-Columbian religions share a number of curious similarities. Be it a raven, a coyote, a hare, or some legendary ancestor, the mythology of nearly every Canadian indigenous group includes the escapades of a Trickster figure, perhaps due to a shared belief that laughter, like smoking and fasting, facilitates communion with the divine. Certain legendary monsters- including hairy giants, massive thunder-making eagles, and huge horned water serpents- feature in native folklore across the country, from the misty jungles of the Pacific to the sunny forests of the Atlantic to the barren tundra of the Arctic. And nearly every Canadian Indian tribe had its shamans, or medicine men, to whom band members turned for healing and advice.

One of the strangest and most widely-held rituals shared by Canadian First Nations involves a structure called a

The Mystery of the Shaking Tent

"Shaking Tent". This ceremonial dwelling consists of a pole frame and a skin covering, similar to the teepee of the prairies and the northern forests, and can be either conical or cylindrical in shape. From the woods of British Columbia to the rocky highlands of Labrador, native medicine men conducted séances in these Shaking Tents, hoping to commune with spirits for the purpose of clairvoyance. During this ritual, the shaman elected to preside over the ceremony fell into a trance, the tent began to shake as if buffeted by unearthly winds, and weird lights flickered in the structure's upper aperture, where the medicine man's spirit-body was said to be in counsel with spirits he summoned.

Samuel de Champlain's Account

The earliest written reference to the ritual of the Shaking Tent appears in French explorer Samuel de Champlain's 1613 book *Les Voyages du Sieur de Champlain,* or "The Voyages of Sir Champlain". A former soldier and spy for King Henry IV of France, Samuel de Champlain, prior to penning his memoirs, had made three voyages to what is now Eastern Canada in the early 1600s for the purpose of establishing a French colony in the Americas and opening up trade with the natives. During the first of these voyages, he explored the lower Laurentian Valley and some of its tributaries. During his second New World expedition, Champlain established a short-lived colony on the shores of what is now Maine, and explored and mapped the Atlantic Coast from what is now Nova Scotia to New England. During his third expedition, launched in 1608, he founded a fur trading fort at the site of what is now Quebec City and established a trading relationship with the local Algonquin Indians. As a condition of their alliance, the natives demanded that Champlain, with his sword, armour, and firearm, help them fight against their hereditary enemy, the powerful Iroquois Confederacy, whose warriors haunted the forests south of the St. Lawrence River. Accordingly, the French explorer joined an Algonquin war party and ventured into enemy territory in the summer of 1609.

While on the war path with his Algonquin allies, Champlain witnessed a Shaking Tent ceremony in which an Algonquin "*Pilotois*", or medicine man, attempted to ascertain the size of the Iroquois war party his tribesmen would soon engage in battle.

"One of these [*Pilotois*] builds a cabin," Champlain wrote, "surrounds it with small pieces of wood, and covers it with his robe: after it is built, he places himself inside, so as not to be seen at all, when he seizes and shakes one of the posts of his cabin, muttering some words between his teeth, by which he says he invokes the devil... This *Pilotois* lies prostrate on the ground, motionless, only speaking with the devil: on a sudden, he rises to his feet, talking, and tormenting himself in such a manner that, although naked, he is all of a perspiration."

The Mystery of the Shaking Tent

Although Champlain's Algonquin friends told him that the tent's movement was the work of spirits, the explorer claimed that he had witnessed the shaman grab one of the tent poles and shake the structure himself.

"They told me also that I should see fire come out from the top," Champlain continued, "which I did not see at all. These rogues counterfeit also their voice, so that it is heavy and clear, and speak in a language unknown to the other savages... the savages think that the devil is speaking..."

Following the ceremony, Champlain and his companions continued up the Richelieu River to what is now Lake Champlain and proceeded south to the site of what would become either Fort Ticonderoga or Crown Point, New York, where they encountered a much larger Iroquois war party. During the battle that ensued, Champlain and one of his French companions shot two Iroquois war chiefs to death with their arquebuses- long matchlock firearms with which these Iroquois were probably unacquainted. Disheartened by the sudden and spectacular deaths of their leaders, the Iroquois broke off the attack and retreated into the woods.

Father Paul Le Jeune's Account

Although Samuel de Champlain made no attempt to hide his skepticism of the ritual of the Shaking Tent, claiming that Indian medicine men routinely pulled such stunts in order to retain the respect of their fellow tribesmen, many Jesuit missionaries who witnessed the phenomenon in the wake of Champlain's explorations were less quick to dismiss it as a shamanic hoax.

One of the first Jesuits to pry into the secret of the Shaking Tent was Father Paul Le Jeune, a former Huguenot, or French Protestant, who converted to Catholicism, joined the Society of Jesus, and rose through its ranks to become the Superior of the Jesuit Mission in New France. During the winter of 1633/34, Le Jeune travelled with a band of Montagnais (Innu) Indians through the northern Appalachian Mountains south of the St. Lawrence River, breaking trails with them on snowshoe and sharing their smoky wigwams at night. He documented his experience in the 1634 issue, or Volume VI, of the *Jesuit Relations*, the *Relations* being reports written by 17th Century Jesuit missionaries for their superiors describing their attempts to convert the natives of New France to Catholicism.

"Towards nightfall," Le Jeune wrote, "two or three young men erected a tent in the middle of our Cabin; they stuck six poles deep into the ground in the form of a circle, and to hold them in place they fastened to the tops of these poles a large ring, which completely encircled them; this done, they enclosed this Edifice with [Blankets], leaving the top of the tent open; it is all that a tall man can to do reach the top of this round tower, capable of holding 5 or 6 men standing upright."

The Mystery of the Shaking Tent

Once the Shaking Tent was erected, the natives extinguished all the fires in their wigwam and threw the embers outside so as to not frighten the spirits that were to enter the tent. After sealing the entrance, the band's shaman began to moan and rock the tent. "Then," wrote Le Jeune, "becoming animated little by little, he commenced to whistle in a hollow tone, and as if it came from afar; then to talk as if in a bottle; to cry like the owls of these countries, which it seems to me have stronger voices than those of France; then to howl and sing, constantly varying the tones; ending by these syllables, *ho ho, hi hi, guigui, nioue,* and other similar sounds, disguising his voice so that it seemed to me I heard those puppets which the showmen exhibit in France."

As the ceremony progressed, the tent began to shake with increasing violence until Le Jeune was sure that the structure would disintegrate. "I was astonished at a man having so much strength," wrote the Jesuit of the medicine man, whom he credited with the shaking, "for, after he had once begun to shake [the tent], he did not stop until the consultation was over, which lasted about three hours".

Of course, since all light had been extinguished from the tent at the beginning of the ritual, Le Jeune could not be certain of the shaman's actions. The natives who also took part in the ceremony assured him that their medicine man was lying on the ground throughout the whole ordeal, his soul having left his body to commune with the newly-arrived spirit visitors at the top of the tent. "Look up!" they urged him. The Frenchman did, and sure enough he saw fiery sparks issuing from tent opening.

When the voice of the shaman announced that the spirits had indeed arrived, the natives in the tent began asking the entities questions about the weather and the location of big game. Each of their inquiries was answered by a strange voice, which Le Jeune accredited to the shaman.

Father Paul Le Jeune wrote on the subject of the Shaking Tent again three years later, in his 1637 *Relations*. In this discourse, he admitted that he now doubted that the phenomenon was simply the product of shamanic trickery, and had come to suspect that it might constitute the work of demons.

The Jesuit's change of heart was attributable in part to the obstinacy with which natives defended the legitimacy of their ritual, and in part to his own experiences in the camp of the Montagnais. Members of his congregation "protested… that it was not the Sorcerer who moved this edifice," Le Jeune wrote, "but a strong wind which suddenly and violently rushed in. And, as proof of this, they told me that the Tent is sometimes so firm that a man can hardly move it, 'Yet thou wilt see it, if thou pleasest to be present there, shake and bend from one side to the other, with such violence and for so long a time, that thou wilt be compelled to confess that there is no human strength that could cause this movement'.

The Mystery of the Shaking Tent

"While passing the winter with the Savages," the missionary continued, "I saw them perform this devilry; I saw strong young men sweat in erecting this Tent; I saw it shake, not with the violence they say it does, but forcibly enough, and for so long a time that I was surprised that a man had strength enough to endure such exertion...

"Furthermore, those whom I have just named, and others, have stoutly asserted to me that the top of this Tent, seven feet high or thereabout, is sometimes bent even to the ground, so powerfully is it agitated. Also, that the arms and legs of the Sorcerer, who was stretched upon the ground, were sometimes seen to emerge at the bottom of the Tent, while the top was shaking violently. They say that the Demon or the wind which enters this little house rushes in with such force, and so disturbs the sorcerer, making him think he is going to fall into an abyss, the earth appearing to open under him, that he emerges in terror from his Tent, which goes on shaking for some time after he has left it."

Le Jeune went on to describe a tale, told to him by a young Indian, which contended that a medicine man who performed the ritual the previous autumn levitated to the top of the tent during the ceremony. This extraordinary event was purportedly witnessed by curious onlookers who lifted the tent's covering and peered inside while the procedure was underway. The medicine man "was heard to fall down," Le Jeune wrote, "uttering a plaintive cry like a man who feels the shock of a fall. Having emerged from these enchantments, he said that he did not know where he had been or what had taken place."

The Experience of Alexander Henry the Elder

In the year 1760, Great Britain emerged victorious from the Seven Years' War, the last of the four great global conflicts to spill into North America throughout the 17th and 18th Centuries. In the ensuing Treaty of Paris, France, for the first time in history, ceded its most important North American holdings to the British Crown.

In the wake of this historic development, an ambitious young Englishman named Alexander Henry purchased an outfit of trading goods and travelled by canoe to the *Pays d'en Haut*, or "Upper Country"- the sparsely populated region surrounding the Great Lakes, which had hitherto been the exclusive domain of Jesuit missionaries, French-Canadian fur traders, and various First Nations. Henry optimistically hoped to inaugurate a trading relationship with Ojibwa and Ottawa Nations who had, only several years prior, fought alongside their French allies against the English in the Seven Years War. Following Henry's perilous voyage into the heart of the Upper Country, British troops began to occupy old French-Canadian fur trading forts throughout the region in an effort to solidify British sovereignty in the area. These British newcomers, who knew far less about the region's

The Mystery of the Shaking Tent

natives than the Frenchmen they displaced, infuriated the Indians of the Great Lakes with their haughty demeanours, their lack of gift-giving, and the trading restrictions they imposed, prompting a coalition of First Nations to launch a series of attacks on British forts in what would become known as Pontiac's Rebellion.

At the outbreak of this conflict, Alexander Henry was trading at Fort Michilimackinac, an old French fur trading fort located at the northern tip of Michigan's Lower Peninsula. The local Ojibwa, who had secretly decided to participate in Pontiac's Rebellion, concocted a brilliant plan to capture the fort by surprise. First, they lured most of the British soldiers outside the fort by inviting them to watch a lacrosse game that they held in an adjacent field on the pretext of celebrating King George III's birthday. While the soldiers were distracted by the Indian athletics, a handful of Ojibwa women inconspicuously made their way towards the fort's open gates, concealing bundles of knives and tomahawks beneath blankets that they wore around their shoulders. When the women were in place, one of the athletes lobbed the lacrosse ball over the fort's walls, prompting the entire Ojibwa team to stampede through the fort's gate. As they entered the fort, the warriors seized the weapons that their women had smuggled inside and proceeded to slaughter or capture every Englishman they found therein. Henry survived the massacre by hiding in the attic of a French-

Canadian fur trader's house. He was discovered several days later by Ojibwa warriors and made prisoner.

Henry spent the better part of 1763 living among the Ojibwa, spared from the more harrowing experiences suffered by his fellow prisoners, many of whom were murdered and cannibalized, due to his adoption by an Ojibwa chief whom he had befriended prior to the massacre. In early 1764, Henry escaped from his captors and travelled with a trio of French-Canadian voyageurs to the fur trading post at Sault Ste. Marie. There, he fell in with another band of Ojibwa who had just received a summons from British military commander Sir William Johnson. The general, desirous of bringing an end to Pontiac's Rebellion, had invited the representatives of all the Great Lakes tribes to attend a great peace conference on the shores of the Niagara River. In order to determine whether or not they ought to attend this council, the Ojibwa attempted to commune with a deity they called the 'Great Turtle'. And thus, a hundred and thirty years after father Le Jeune's adventure, Alexander Henry bore witness to the phenomenon of the Shaking Tent.

"For invoking and consulting the Great Turtle," Henry wrote, "the first thing to be done was the building of a large house or wigwam, within which was placed a species of tent for the use of the priest and reception of the spirit. The tent was formed of moose-skins, hung over a framework of wood. Five poles, or rather pillars, of five different species of timber, about ten feet in height and eight inches in diameter

The Mystery of the Shaking Tent

were set in a circle of about four feet in diameter. The holes made to receive them were about two feet deep; and the pillars being set, the holes were filled up again, with the earth which had been dug out. At top the pillars were bound together by a circular hoop, or girder. Over the whole of this edifice were spread the moose-skins, covering it at top and round the sides, and made fast with thongs of the same; except that on one side a part was left unfastened, to admit the entrance of the priest."

At nightfall, while the whole band stood by in anticipation, the medicine man chosen to preside over the ceremony emerged half-naked from his wigwam. The shaman walked over to the tent and crawled through the entrance. "His head was scarcely within side when the edifice," wrote Henry, "massy as it has been described, began to shake; and the skins were no sooner let fall than the sounds of numerous voices were heard beneath them, some yelling, some barking as dogs, some howling like wolves; and in this horrible concert were mingled screams and sobs, as of despair, anguish, and the sharpest pain. Articulate speech was also uttered, as if from human lips; but in a tongue unknown to the audience. After some time these confused and frightful noises were succeeded by a perfect silence; and now a voice not heard before seemed to manifest the arrival of a new character in the tent. This was a low and feeble voice, resembling the cry of a young puppy. The sound was no sooner distinguished, than all the Indians clapped their hands for joy, exclaiming that this was the Chief Spirit, the Turtle, the spirit that never lied. Other voices which they had discriminated from time to time they had previously hissed, as recognizing them to belong to evil and lying spirits, which deceive mankind."

Throughout the half hour that followed, a variety of songs issued from the tent, each of them sung by a different voice. Finally, once the last song died out, the medicine man called out from inside the tent that the Great Turtle was ready to answer any questions the Indians might have for him.

The band's chief asked whether the English planned to attack them, and whether there were many English troops assembled at Fort Niagara, the site of the scheduled rendezvous. "These questions having been put by the priest," Henry wrote, "the tent instantly shook; and for some seconds after it continued to rock so violently that I expected to see it levelled with the ground. All this was a prelude, as I supposed, to the answers to be given; but a terrific cry announced, with sufficient intelligibility, the departure of the Turtle."

All of a sudden, the tent fell silent. The Ojibwa spectators waited with bated breath for the spirit's reply. About fifteen minutes later, the tent shook again, and the tremulous voice of the Great Turtle began babbling in a language which none of the onlookers could understand. Once the spirit had delivered its incompressible report, the medicine man, who apparently understood every word,

The Mystery of the Shaking Tent

informed those assembled that the Great Turtle had flown across Lake Huron and over the easterly forest to Fort Niagara, where he found few Englishmen. He proceeded down the length of Lake Ontario and further down the St. Lawrence River to Montreal, where he found a huge fleet of ships filled with British soldiers.

The chief then asked the Great Turtle whether Sir William Johnson would receive them as friends. "Sir William Johnson," the medicine man replied, interpreting the words of the spirit, "will fill their canoes with presents; with blankets, kettles, guns, gunpowder and shot, and large barrels of rum such as the stoutest of the Indians will not be able to lift; and every man will return in safety to his family." At this, the assemblage cheered, and many warriors declared their intention to attend the meeting at Fort Niagara.

The natives proceeded to ask the spirit questions about distant friends and the fate of sick family members. Henry himself, despite his skepticism, presented the Great Turtle with the customary gift of tobacco before asking whether he would ever see his native country again. The spirit replied that he would. Indeed, Henry would go on to survive Pontiac's rebellion and make three voyages to his native England.

Paul Kane's Account

Alexander Henry the Elder was the first of the so-called 'pedlars'- independent Montreal-based English and Scottish fur traders who took over the old trading grounds of the French in the wake of the British conquest of Canada. In 1789, a handful of these pedlars established the North West Company, a fur trading enterprise which, from its inception, found itself locked in fierce competition with the powerful Hudson's Bay Company which dominated the watershed of the great northerly bay for which it was named. In the tradition of the *coureurs des bois* who first brought the fur trade to the territories they inherited, the men of the North West Company began making long canoe trips deep into the wilderness to seek out new native trading partners, leaving the Hudson's Bay Company to conduct its own business, as one disgruntled HBC employee put it, "asleep by the frozen sea". These inland voyages sparked an age of discovery in which both the North West Company and the Hudson's Bay Company launched major exploratory expeditions west and north for the purpose of extending the reach of their respective enterprises. During these operations, explorers found that the Shaking Tent ceremony was practiced in even the most remote corners of the interior. In January 1793, for example, HBC explorer Peter Fidler witnessed a Shaking Tent ceremony in the foothills of the Rocky Mountains in which a Blackfoot medicine man correctly ascertained the fate of two braves who had travelled south on a diplomatic mission to the Shoshone tribe, accurately predicting the date of their return.

By the time the two great Canadian fur trading associations amalgamated in 1821 under the umbrella of the HBC, their industry had expanded into the heart of the Canadian interior. From the Atlantic to the Pacific, most of the Hudson's Bay Company's southerly trading posts were connected by a great trans-continental trail stretching from York Factory- the HBC's New World headquarters on Hudson Bay- and Fort William- the North West Company's field headquarters on Lake Superior- across the Canadian prairies and over the Canadian Rockies to the Columbia River and the Pacific Coast beyond. Twice a year, a fur brigade called the Columbia Express followed this trail west, bearing trade goods, letters, equipment, and provisions for the forts of the interior. Another brigade, called the York Factory Express, made similar biannual journeys east over the same trail, carrying furs for the European market.

Undoubtedly, the most vivid picture of this trans-continental fur route was that painted, both literally and literarily, by a 19th Century Irish-Canadian artist named Paul Kane. While on his Grand Tour of Europe- an essential element of any serious 19th Century painter's education- 34-year-old Kane met George Catlin, an American artist who had spent the past decade travelling up and down the Mississippi and Missouri Rivers, painting portraits of the Native Americans he met along the way. Many of the subjects of

Catlin's paintings had only recently been introduced to Euro-American society, and practiced ancient ways of life which Catlin suspected were fast-disappearing.

Kane was deeply impressed by Catlin and his work, and adopted his philosophy that it was the artist's duty to illustrate these dying cultures for the sake of posterity. Inspired by the American artist, Kane decided to undertake a similar project in Canada. From 1846 to 1848, he explored the Canadian West by way of the trans-continental fur trail, sketching the scenes and characters he encountered along the way. He participated in Metis buffalo hunts on the Canadian prairies, crossed the continental divide twice on snowshoe, shot the rapids of the Columbia River, and canoed the Salish Sea with the natives of Vancouver Island, becoming a sideline witness to several historic battles and massacres along the way.

Following his epic journey across the continent and back, Kane was commissioned to render over a hundred and twenty of the field sketches he produced into oil paintings. In 1859, he included some of his masterpieces in his book *'Wanderings of an Artist Among the Indians of North America'*, a travel memoir based on his adventures in the Canadian wilds.

Of all of Kane's many colourful experiences on the Canadian frontier, perhaps the strangest took place near the end of his return journey, when the Cree and Saulteaux

The Mystery of the Shaking Tent

Indians with whom the artist travelled performed the ritual of the Shaking Tent.

Kane described the event in his memoirs, recording that it took place on the night of July 24th, 1848, while he and his travelling companions were waiting out a storm on the shores of Lake Winnipeg.

"In the evening," he wrote, "our Indians constructed a jonglerie, or medicine lodge, the main object of which was to procure a fair wind for next day. For this purpose they first drive ten or twelve poles, nine or ten feet long, into the ground, enclosing a circular area of about three feet in diameter, with a boat sail open at the top. The medicine-man, one of whom is generally found in every brigade, gets inside and commences shaking the poles violently, rattling his medicinal rattle, and singing hoarse incantations to the Great Spirit for a fair wind. Being unable to sleep on account of the discordant noises, I wrapped a blanket round me, and went out into the woods... and lay down amongst those on the outside of the medicine lodge, to witness the proceedings. I had no sooner done so than the incantations at once ceased, and the performer exclaimed that a white man was present. How he ascertained this fact I am at a loss to surmise, as it was pitch dark at the time, and he was enclosed in the narrow tent, without any apparent opening through which he could espy me, even had it been light enough to distinguish one person from another...

"After about two hours' shaking and singing, the medicine-man cried out that he saw five boats with the sails set running before the wind, which communication was greeted by the whole party with their usual grunt of satisfaction and assent.

"After this, many questions were asked him by the Indians, some inquiring after the health of their families at home, whom they had not seen for many months. Upon putting the question, the inquirer threw a small piece of tobacco over the covering of the tent, upon which the medicine-man agitated the tent, and shook his rattle violently, and then replied that he saw one family enjoying themselves over a fat sturgeon, another engaged in some pleasing employment, &c. &c. I then put a question to him myself, accompanying it with a double portion of tobacco, for which I got a double portion of noise." Kane asked about the fate of the souvenirs he had acquired throughout the course of his journey- artifacts like the trophy head of a buffalo bull he had shot, a bears' claw necklace given to him by an Assiniboine chief, and a Flathead Indian skull he had stolen from a burial ground- which he had been obliged to entrust to a coureur. "The medicine man told me," Kane wrote, "that he saw the party with my baggage encamped on a sandy point, which we had ourselves passed two days before.

"However singular the coincidence may appear, it is a fact, that on the next day we had a fair wind, for which the medicine-man of course took all the credit; and it is no less true, that the canoes with my baggage were on the sandy point on the day stated, for I inquired particularly of them when they came up to us."

One of Kane's companions on the last leg of his journey was an old Hudson's Bay Company trader and Napoleonic War veteran named Major Donald McKenzie. The old *engagé*, as HBC employees were sometimes called, had seen many strange things in the camps of the Indians throughout the course of his long service for the Company. He had attended many a Shaking Tent ceremony, and had heard some disturbing tales about the ritual from the French-Canadian voyageurs with whom he rubbed shoulders.

"The Major," Kane wrote, "who, with many other intelligent persons, is a firm believer in the Indians' medicine, told me that a Canadian once had the temerity to peep under the covering which enclosed the jonglerie, but that he got such a fright that he never fairly recovered from it, nor could he ever be prevailed upon to tell what it was that had so appalled him."

Bishop Mountain's Story

Another description of the Shaking Tent ritual, which is roughly contemporaneous with Kane's, is that which appears in the writings of George J. Mountain, the third Anglican Bishop of Quebec. Two years before the commencement of Kane's journey west, Bishop Mountain, under the auspices of a British Protestant evangelical organization called the Church Mission Society, travelled from Montreal to the Red River Valley in what is now southern Manitoba. The Valley was an important Hudson's Bay Company district, home to Orcadian and Scottish settlers, Cree and Saulteaux Indians, and a large population of Metis- the people born of country marriages between French-Canadian voyageurs and native women.

On the way to the Valley, Bishop Mountain came across the skeletal frames of old derelict Shaking Tents, which he described as being "formed of young saplings, or single branches stripped of the leaves and twigs, the whole encircled at intervals by bands or hoops of the same material, and covered with dressed kins, of considerable height; but only of a size to admit one man..."

During his stay in the Red River Valley, Bishop Mountain wrote three letters to the Church Mission Society in which he described the route to the region, the spiritual state of the Valley's inhabitants, and the headway made by Anglican missionaries in their efforts to draw local natives into the fold of the Church of England. These letters were later compiled and published in London, England, under the title *The Journal of the Bishop of Montreal During a Visit to the Church Missionary Society's North-West America Mission.*

Although Bishop Mountain never had the opportunity of personally witnessing the Shaking Tent ceremony during his sojourn, he was informed of its particulars by two former Cree medicine men who had since converted to Anglicanism. In his third letter to the Church Mission Society, Mountain wrote that, according to his informants, the shamans who perform the ritual lie prostrate at the bottom of the tent with "their hands and feet tied by hard knots, which they contrive, by some trick, to disengage. While they are lying in the tent, it becomes violently agitated, the top swinging rapidly backward and forward in the view of the spectators on the outside, who also hear a variety of 'strange sounds and voices, unlike the voice of man'". With the help of the "aerial visitants" to whom these voices are attributed, the shaman is able to "learn news respecting persons and affairs at a great distance", and to inflict "disease and death upon persons some hundred miles off, whether his own enemies or those of his neighbours who have recourse to his magical skill". Although the medicine man will never dare to look directly at the roof of the tent during the ceremony, he can sometimes, out of the corner of his eye, glimpse tiny starlike orbs of light floating near the tent's uppermost hoop.

J.G. Kohl's Story

In 1855, a German travel writer named Johann Georg Kohl spent time among the Ojibwa of Lake Superior, exploring the Indian camps and villages scattered throughout the Apostle Islands in the lake's southwestern corner and traversing the Keweenaw Peninsula from its tip to the innermost heart of Keweenaw Bay, the site of a remote Indian Mission. In 1859, an English-language account of his adventure was published in London, England, under the title *Kitchi-gami: Wanderings Around Lake Superior*.

In his book, Kohl explained the ritual of the Shaking Tent as it was described to him by a French-Canadian voyageur who had lived among the Ojibwa, and who was married to an Ojibwa woman.

"The lodge which their jossakids, or prophets, or, as the Canadians term them, 'jongleurs,' erect for their incantations," Kohl wrote, "is composed of stout posts, connected with basket-work, and covered with birch bark. It is tall and narrow, and resembles a chimney. It is very firmly built, and two men, even if exerting their utmost strength, would be unable to move, shake, or bend it. It is so narrow that a man who crawls in has but scanty space to move about in it."

"Thirty years ago," Kohl's informant claimed, "I was present at the incantation and performance of a jossakid in one of these lodges. I saw the man creep into the hut, which was about ten feet high, after swallowing a mysterious potion made from a root. He immediately began singing and beating a drum in his basket-work chimney. The entire case began gradually trembling and shaking, and oscillating slowly amid great noise. The more the necromancer sang and drummed,

The Mystery of the Shaking Tent

the more violent the oscillations of the long case became. It bent back and forwards, up and down, like the mast of a vessel caught in a storm and tossed on the waves. I could not understand how these movements could be produced by a man inside, as we could not have caused them from the exterior.

"The drum ceased, and the jossakid yelled that 'the spirits were coming over him.' We then heard through the noise, and cracking, and oscillations of the hut, two voices speaking inside, one above, the other below. The lower one asked questions, which the upper one answered.

"Both voices seemed entirely different, and I believed I could explain them by very clever ventriloquism. Some spiritualists among us, however, explained it through modern spiritualism..."

Roughly thirty years after the incident, not long before Kohl's trip to Lake Superior, the voyageur found the jossakid on his deathbed. In his old age, the medicine man had renounced the pagan rites of his ancestors and resolved to die a Christian. Hoping to take advantage of this singular situation, Kohl's informant asked the old Indian how he had managed to make the tent shake and produce the unearthly voices on that strange night thirty years prior. "Now is the time to confess all truthfully," he said. "Tell me, then, how and through what means thou didst decieve us?"

"I know it," the old Indian replied. "I have become a Christian, I am old, I am sick, I cannot live much longer, and

I can do no other than speak the truth. Believe me, I did not decieve you at that time. I did not move the lodge. It was shaken by the power of the spirits. Nor did I speak with a double tongue. I only repeated to you what the spirits told me. I heard their voices. The top of the lodge was full of them, and before me the sky and wide lands lay expanded. I could see a great distance around me, and believeed I could recognize the most distant objects."

"The old dying jossakid said this with such an expression of simple truth and firm conviction," the voyageur told Kohl, "that it seemed, to me, at least, that he did not consider himself a deceiver, and believed in the efficacy of his magic arts and the reality of his visions."

Cecil Denny's Account

On July 1st, 1867, the British colonies of Nova Scotia, New Brunswick, and the Province of Canada (i.e. Ontario and Quebec) were united into a single federation, the Dominion of Canada. The Dominion's first prime minister, Sir John A. Macdonald, hoped to combine his fledgling country with the westerly Colony of British Columbia, forming an immense continental Dominion stretching from the Atlantic to the Pacific. In order to accomplish this end, he would have to connect Canada with British Columbia by means of a transcontinental railroad, and in order to build that iron thoroughfare, he would first have to bring British law and order to the territory that lay in between- a vast and wild domain known as Rupert's Land.

Although the Hudson's Bay Company nominally held sway over Rupert's Land- a territory named after its first benefactor, Prince Rupert of the Rhine- the prairies, badlands, and sandhills between the North Saskatchewan River and the American border were, in reality, dominated by two rival Indian alliances: the Blackfoot Confederacy and the Iron Confederacy.

The Blackfoot, whom several 19th Century writers designated the most warlike tribe on the northern half of the continent, were composed of four nations united by blood ties and a common language: the Siksika, the Blood, the Northern Peigan, and the Southern Piegan. The Iron Confederacy, on the other hand, was an alliance composed of the unrelated Plains Cree, Assiniboine, Saulteaux, and Stoney- long-time trading partners of the Hudson's Bay Company who served as middlemen in the fur trade.

Macdonald knew that the Dominion of Canada had neither the men nor the resources to tame Rupert's Land by force, as the U.S. Army was attempting to do in the American West. If it hoped to put an end to the roving, thievery, and violence that characterized life on the Canadian plains and produce in them an environment hospitable to the construction of a railroad, it would need to foster law and order on the plains in a firm yet tactful manner, through the use of a mounted police force.

Ever conscious of his meagre budget, Prime Minister Macdonald delayed the formation of such a police force throughout his entire first term. In early 1870, he began receiving disturbing reports from Hudson's Bay Company officers and his own federal agents that American traders were beginning to establish heavily-fortified trading posts on Canadian soil, in the region through which he hoped to build his railroad. Having taken advantage of a loophole in American law, these businessmen were selling rotgut whisky to the Canadian Indians in exchange for buffalo robes, rapidly depressing the once-powerful Blackfoot and Iron Confederacies into nations of starvelings and alcoholics. Macdonald realized that he would need to act quickly to establish Canadian sovereignty in the region if he hoped to keep it from being annexed by the land-hungry United States, which was constantly expanding its frontiers in accordance with the concept of Manifest Destiny. Still, he prolonged the inevitable.

In 1873, after learning of the whisky-fuelled Cypress Hills Massacre, Macdonald knew that he could delay no longer. With the help of Canadian Parliament, he approved the formation of a 300-man force of mounted policemen that year. After a winter of relentless drilling, this force, styled the North-West Mounted Police, made a gruelling trek from Manitoba across the Canadian prairies to what is now

The Mystery of the Shaking Tent

southwest Alberta. From Fort Macleod, their first permanent headquarters on the banks of the Oldman River, these Mounties brought a peaceful end to the whisky trade, engratiated themselves with the local Blackfoot, and successfully established law and order on the Canadian plains.

Among the first officers of the North-West Mounted Police was an Englishman named Cecil Edward Denny. Born into a family of old aristocratic stock, Denny had immigrated to the United States at the age of 19 in search of adventure. He relocated to Canada in 1874, joined the North-West Mounted Police as a constable, and quickly climbed the rungs of the para-martial ladder until he obtained the rank of Sub-Inspector. He participated in the Long March west across the prairies, assisted in the establishment of Fort Macleod, and oversaw the construction of what would become Fort Calgary. In 1877, he attended the Treaty 7 negotiations at Blackfoot Crossing, and played a key role in settling the various Blackfoot nations onto reserves in the aftermath of that conference.

In his writings, Denny reported having several extraordinary experiences during his years on the Canadian plains, claiming to have seen the ghostly apparition of a Cree village whose inhabitants were massacred by the Blackfoot long ago, and to have witnessed many inexplicable feats performed by Blackfoot medicine men.

One of the strangest of Denny's experiences took place on a moonlit night in the summer of 1879, on the banks of the Red Deer River in what is now central Alberta. That evening, the Mountie pitched his tent near a Blackfoot Indian camp and decided to pay a visit to the band's medicine man. Accompanied by his interpreter, Billy Gladstone- an American carpenter who had worked for the Hudson's Bay Company, American whisky traders, and the North-West Mounted Police- Denny walked along the riverbank to the medicine man's teepee, which was pitched a short distance from the main camp. He described what happened next in his article *Blackfoot Magic*, which was published posthumously in the September 1944 issue of the magazine *The Beaver*, writing the following:

"We entered the lodge, which had only a small fire burning in the centre. The medicine man was sitting wrapped in his buffalo robe at the head of the teepee, smoking one of their long medicine pipes. He paid no attention to us whatever. I therefore sat down near him, lighting my own pipe and, placing a present of two plugs of tobacco near him, proceeded to smoke quietly, without a sign of recognition being made by the Indian.

"Everything was very still in the lodge, while outside in the main camp drums could be heard beating in different parts, wherever dances were being held. We had sat this way for quite a time, when I was startled by the sound of a bell ringing above me, over the top of the lodge. I could see

The Mystery of the Shaking Tent

nothing, and the Indian made no move. Presently the teepee itself began to rock, even lifting off the ground a foot or more behind me. When it is remembered that a large Indian tent consists of dozens of long poles crossed at the top, wide apart at the bottom, and covered with buffalo hides, it will seem that it is nearly impossible to lift one side, for no wind can blow them over.

"The rocking motion ceased after a while, and I went outside the lodge to see if anyone had been playing tricks; but not a human being was in sight near us, the moon was clear, and you could see a long distance. On returning and resuming my seat after a short interval, the tent again began to rock, and so violently that it would sometimes lift several feet on one side, so that you could plainly see outside. My interpreter was thoroughly frightened by this time, and I was not much better, but the Indian never stirred. However we had seen enough and left, returning to our camp thoroughly mystified."

A.G. Black's Story

In 1881, the first ties of the great trans-continental railroad envisioned by Sir John A. Macdonald were laid at the town of Bonfield, Ontario. Four years later, the last spike of the Canadian Pacific Railway was hammered home at Craigellachie, British Columbia, ushering in a new era of settlement in Western Canada. Following the subsequent influx of homesteaders into the so-called 'Last Best West', the Canadian government banned many traditional First Nations ceremonies, from the Sun Dance of the Blackfoot to the Potlatch of the Coast Salish, in an effort to assimilate the country's indigenous peoples into the Euro-Canadian culture that was sweeping across the continent, rapidly displacing that of their ancestors.

Despite the best efforts of the Canadian government, the Shaking Tent ceremony continued to be practiced on the fringes of settler society, in the wilder reaches of the Canadian frontier, well into the 20th Century. In July 1929, for example, this necromantic rite was performed by an Ojibwa shaman near the Whitesands First Nations Reserve just northwest of Ontario's Lake Nipigon. A.G. Black, the manager of the Hudson's Bay Company's proximate trading post, Nipigon House, described the event in an article for the December 1934 issue of the magazine *The Beaver*, entitled 'Shaking the Wigwam'.

That day, Black and his fellow traders set up camp near the Whitesands Reserve and unpacked their wares. They had timed their visit so that it coincided with that of the band's Indian agent, knowing that the local Ojibwa would be eager to spend their newly-delivered treaty money on ammunition, groceries, calico, and other HBC goods.

After a busy day of trading, the traders decided to pay a visit to the band's medicine man, a shriveled old shaman

The Mystery of the Shaking Tent

named August, and see if he would perform the old Shaking Tent ceremony for them. In lieu of the traditional payment of tobacco, the traders presented the conjuror with $15, equivalent to about $220 Canadian ($160 USD) today. The fee was sufficient, and the band members, at August's request, eagerly set about collecting the requisite materials for the ancient ritual.

"Before dusk," Black wrote, "two Indian lads went to the bush to get the necessary willow poles, which were driven fast into the ground and fastened with two willow hoops, one in the centre and the other tapering the poles at the top. The poles were tested by nearly all present, and were found immovable. A can of shot was tied to the top of the poles, and the birch bark was then fastened on to the outside to complete the construction.

"As it darkened and the moon came up, the Indians squatted in a circle around the wigwam at a distance of four or six feet from it. A small opening was made in the wigwam for the Indian to crawl in, and closed immediately on his entrance. The wigwam commenced to shake as soon as the Indian disappeared, and the can of shot began to rattle."

The old medicine man broke into eerie tune which sent shivers through the onlookers. Immediately, as if prompted by the music, the structure began to shake. The shaking and singing continued for nearly half an hour, when suddenly, a strange voice was heard at the top of the wigwam. The medicine man replied to the unintelligible utterance, his voice sounding from the base of the tent. "The voices," Black wrote, "were decidedly different."

After conversing with the strange voice for some time, August told the native onlookers that they were welcome to ask any questions they pleased. The old medicine man was subsequently bombarded with all sorts of queries, most of them pertaining to fishing and trapping, which he answered one by one, always first consulting with the strange voice.

"When the natives' questions become fewer," Black wrote, "August said he would be glad to answer any questions asked by the white onlookers. At the suggestions of the others, I asked 'May we hold the wigwam while it is shaking?' A rapid talk by August commenced in the wigwam and I could feel an unpleasantness among the Indians about me. Although I could not understand their language at the time, I sensed something was wrong, and I was told that August had said that if the white people interfered with the motion of the wigwam he would make such a big wind it would blow people and houses into the lake." In order to avoid trouble with the medicine man, Black recanted his question.

August then announced that he would summon the spirit of a bear into the structure, and fight it. "The fight began," Black wrote, "and this is where I received my greatest surprise. The Indians seated around yelled to August 'an-ahuck' (get stronger). The top of the wigwam bent until it

The Mystery of the Shaking Tent

nearly touched the ground during the fight." Eventually, the shaman killed the spirit bear, and repeated a similar performance with the spirit of a lynx.

At dawn, the shaking stopped, and August emerged from the structure. The medicine man's face was covered with beads of sweat, which seemed to Black more accordant with the sort of perspiration one would exude as a result of being enclosed in a birch bark wigwam all night long than the product of several hours of intense physical exertion. "The bark was immediately removed from the wigwam," he wrote, "and we examined the poles and were surprised to find them as solid as they had been at first."

Black finished his article by stating, "I have been informed, although I have not witnessed it, that August can make a teepee shake by merely throwing his hat into it. I hope some day to see him do this!"

Conclusion

Like the vocation of the Indian medicine man, the ritual of the Shaking Tent seems to have died out sometime in the 20th Century, necromancy and divination being at odds with the doctrines of the various Christian denominations to which the members of many First Nations have converted. The extinction of this practice has ensured that modern students of the subject, equipped though they may be with the luxury of hindsight, are no better prepared to tackle the mystery of the Shaking Tent than the 17th, 18th, 19th, and 20th Century witnesses who preserved their memories of the ritual in their writings.

Perhaps, like Samuel de Champlain maintained, the uncanny oscillations of the conjurer's tent, the mysterious lights that flickered at its upper aperture, and the unearthly voices heard therein, constitute little more than clever acts of shamanic deception. Maybe, like Father Le Jeune believed, these unsettling spectacles are the work of unholy demons conjured by Indian sorcerers in league with Satan, wittingly or otherwise. Or perhaps, as generations of Canadian Indians contended, these phenomena are truly the manifestations of benevolent spirits or the souls of the dead. As is true of other marvels effected by the Indian medicine men of yesteryear- such as those which can perhaps best be classified as the frontier versions of firewalking, voodoo dolls, and Houdini's straitjacket escape, of which this author hopes to treat in future articles- the riddle of the Shaking Tent remains one of the many great unsolved mysteries of Canada.

THE OUIJA BOARD OF COBDEN, ONTARIO

SINCE AT LEAST the late 1800s, Western spiritualists have attempted to communicate with the spirits of the dead through so-called 'talking boards'. These devices originally consisted of wooden boards on which were painted the letters of the alphabet, along with an essential accessory called a 'planchette'- a heart-shaped piece of wood with three wheels or felt sliders attached to its underside. During Victorian-era séances, occult practitioners would dim the lights, sit around the talking board, and invite any spirits present to communicate with them. That accomplished, the practitioners would lightly place their fingers on top of the planchette, which would proceed to glide across the surface of the talking board, seemingly of its own accord. Ideally, the planchette would point to a succession of letters which spelled out a coherent message ostensibly attributable to some otherworldly entity.

In the 1890s, four American businessman patented a particular style of talking board which displayed the alphabet, the numbers 0 through 9, and the words 'YES', 'NO', and 'GOOD BYE'. The businessman dubbed their innovation the 'Ouija board', and went on to found the Kenneth Novelty Company, through which they produced and sold these devices on a massive scale. Due to their marketing efforts, the Ouija board quickly metamorphosed from a relatively obscure spiritualist tool into a popular and largely-innocent parlour game. This perception endured until 1973, when the horror film *The Exorcist* hit American theatres, transforming the talking board once again into a sinister apparatus of the occult.

Although most post-1973 accounts of Ouija board use are either tales of scoffing skepticism or dire dissuasion, there are a few pre-*Exorcist* anecdotes involving positive outcomes resultant of Ouija board consultation. One of these appeared in the February 1955 issue of the magazine *Fate*.

Violet Bender of Ottawa, Ontario, the lady who submitted the story, claimed that sometime in the 1880s, her aunt had come into the possession of a talking board. Although Mrs. Bender was not explicit in her description of the apparatus, it seems possible that this particular talking board's planchette was equipped with a pencil.

Violet's aunt used the apparatus to help her compose music. In 1902, her aunt died, and the board was bequeathed to her mother, the wife of an Anglican clergyman.

The Ouija Board of Cobden, Ontario

Violet's eldest sister, Winnifred, who was eighteen years old at the time, quickly discovered that the board would write for her. "It provided her with many hours of amusement," Violet wrote. "Her girl friends came to ask about their beaux. It replied equally well to mental questions-that is, to unspoken questions in a person's mind. Whoever had the strongest will or the greatest power of concentration got the reply to his or her question."

At that time, Violet and her family lived in the village of Cobden, Ontario, situated on an old and well-used portage route circumventing a set of rapids on the Ottawa River. Word quickly spread throughout Cobden, as it so often does in small communities, that Winnifred could locate lost or stolen articles using her Ouija board.

Early one morning, Violet and her family awoke to the frantic ringing of the rectory bell; someone, it seemed, desperately wanted to see the minister. Violet's father threw open the rectory window and stuck out his head. "Who is there?" he called. "What do you want?"

"We want to ask that board of your daughter's a question," came the reply.

"Well," the minister said with some reproach, "four o'clock in the morning is a queer time to come to ask a question."

The visitor replied that his little girl was lost in the woods, and that a search party had been hunting for her all night, but to no avail.

Violet's father told the man that he would do what he could. He roused Winnifred, informed her of the situation, and asked her to use her talking board to determine the girl's location. Afraid of what the answer might be, Winnifred asked the question and put her hands on the planchette. The board gave the following reply:

"THE CHILD IS SAFE IN A HOUSE NEAR THE TRACK"

Winnifred's father relayed the information to the desperate father, who tore off in the direction of the railroad.

Later that day, the father found his little girl safe and sound in a log cabin near the railway. She had wandered away from her family's farm with some cows, and the family living in the cabin had taken her in.

Thirty years later, Violet Bender was happily married to a clergyman and living not far from Cobden. One evening, she got a call from another clergyman who asked whether she had the talking board and planchette that her family once owned. Violet informed the minister that her eldest sister, Winnifred, had the board, and that she was now married and living in Australia.

The Ouija Board of Cobden, Ontario

"The clergyman," Violet wrote, "then explained that a child was lost in that district, and the people, remembering how over 30 years ago another lost child had been found, wanted to consult the planchette again." The article offered no word regarding the fate of the child.

Rather than end on this note, the author of this piece feels obliged to remind you, dear reader, that this particular anecdote, with its bittersweet denouement, is a bit of an anomaly when it comes to Ouija board stories. Today, popular culture is riddled with cautionary tales expounding the dangers of Ouija board séances, most of them warning that improper use of the device can leave the practitioner vulnerable to attacks by evil spirits or demons. These exhortations are based on the tenets of various Judeo-Christian religious denominations which condemn any attempt to contact the spirit world. Perhaps the most well-known religious denunciation of Ouija board use is that of the Roman Catholic Church, which expounds its position in paragraph 2,116 of the 1992 *Catechism of the Catholic Church*:

"All forms of divination are to be rejected: recourse to Satan or demons, conjuring up the dead or other practices falsely supposed to 'unveil' the future."

The section outlining this doctrine cites two verses from sacred scripture. The first of these is Chapter 18, Verse 10 of the Book of Deuteronomy (the fifth book of the Hebrew Torah, detailing the divine laws revealed to Moses on Mount Sinai), which denounces child sacrifice, fortune telling, soothsaying, divining, spell-casting, consulting ghosts and spirits, or seeking "oracles from the dead". The second passage cited is Chapter 29, Verse 8, of the Book of Jeremiah, which warns against false prophets and diviners who lie and deceive in God's name.

Whether you consider the Ouija board a useful tool, a harmless toy, or a dangerous door to another world, perhaps the wisest policy is to treat it with caution.

CRYPTOZOOLOGY

HARRISON HOT SPRINGS: THE SASQUATCH CAPITAL OF CANADA

I F YOU DRIVE EAST of Chilliwack, British Columbia, take a left on the B.C. Highway 9, cross the Fraser River, and continue north for about ten minutes, you'll enter an enchanting corridor through the Coast Mountains known as the Agassiz-Harrison Valley. This stretch of farmland, flanked by dark green mountains covered from base to peak with thick coniferous jungle, leads to a little village hugging the southern shores of vast Harrison Lake.

If you meander through the streets of this tiny community and keep a vigilant eye, you may begin to realize that there's something distinctly different about the place. For instance, you might notice the hairy sentinel who keeps perpetual watch at the village entrance, lounging contentedly on a wooden bench beneath the town's welcome sign.

The Sasquatch Capital of Canada

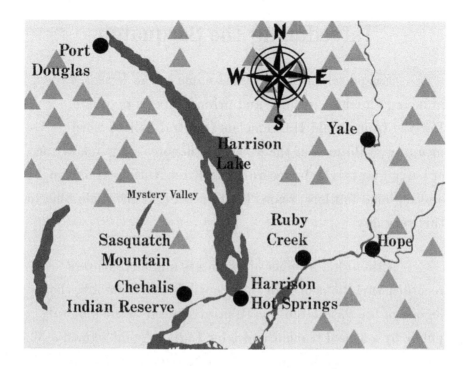

Perhaps you'll catch a glimpse of another more startling village guardian standing further up the road, poised to hurl a wooden boulder at passing cars.

If you're especially observant, you may detect a certain pattern in the titles of various establishments; the names of various inns, liquor stores, and ski resorts hint at a recurring theme. Even the street signs are topped with a stylized silhouette of British Columbia's most elusive resident. Welcome to Harrison Hot Springs, the Sasquatch capital of Canada.

Introducing the Sasquatch

"Sasquatch" is a household name in the Fraser Valley, inducing chuckles in some and primal shivers in others. Derived from an old Halkomelem (Central Salish) word meaning "wild man of the woods", it denotes a legendary race of hairy giants which, according to First Nations tradition and regional folklore, roams the forests of British Columbia to this very day.

Although a number of explorers and adventurers recorded variations of it in their journals and memoirs, the legend of the Sasquatch was first introduced to the general public by a school teacher and later Indian Agent named J.W. Burns, who began teaching at the Chehalis First Nation Reserve- located a mere fifteen minutes from Harrison Hot Springs- in 1925. Burns used the word 'Sasquatch' for the first time in an article published in the April 1, 1929 issue of *Maclean's* magazine, and the name stuck.

The Sasquatch Capital of Canada

Throughout the 1930s and '40s, Burns published a number of accounts of Sasquatch sightings which were reported to him by his Chehalis friends. These sightings took place in the mountainous country surrounding the Chehalis Reserve, from the so-called 'Mystery Valley' west of Harrison Lake to the Sasquatch Cave outside Yale, B.C., far to the east.

The Sasquatch Capital of Canada

Through what is probably sheer coincidence, the epicenter of the various Sasquatch sightings reported by Burns' informants seemed to be Harrison Hot Springs, a resort community renowned for its thermal mineral waters, which had been used by the Chehalis for centuries and discovered by white prospectors during the Fraser River Gold Rush. The village's community fully embraced its newfound status as the Sasquatch capital of Canada and began holding an annual summer festival called 'Sasquatch Days' with the neighbouring residents of the Chehalis Reserve- a cherished tradition which endures to this day.

The Sasquatch of Ruby Creek

Since the publication of Burns' first article, Sasquatch sightings have taken place in the wilderness surrounding Harrison Hot Springs with casual frequency. Perhaps the most famous of these sightings is the one which took place just outside Ruby Creek, a tiny rural community situated on the banks of the Fraser River about 14 kilometres (9 miles) northeast of Harrison Hot Springs, as the crow flies.

In 1941, a Chehalis man named George Chapman lived in a cabin near Ruby Creek with his wife Jeannie and their three children. One day, while George was away from home, working as a tie gang labourer on the nearby railroad, the eldest of the Chapman children ran into cabin and declared that a "cow" had emerged from the woods. Alarmed by the inexplicable panic in her 9-year-old son's tone, Jeannie stepped outside to investigate and spied what she first took to be a grizzly bear ambling along a distant hillside. Her two remaining children, aged 7 and 5, were playing in a nearby field at the time, and did not appear to be in any imminent danger. Nevertheless, Jeannie decided to call her children to the cabin as a precaution.

The bear's strange physical appearance unnerved Jeannie, and so she decided to keep an eye on it from the cabin door as it made its way down the hill towards the railroad. Upon reaching the tracks, the animal, to Jeannie's astonishment, reared up on its hind legs and began to stride towards the cabin like a human. Mrs. Chapman quickly realized that the creature was not a bear at all, but rather an enormous eight-foot-tall man covered with long brown hair. "I had much too much time to look at it," she would later say of the incident. Jeannie described the giant has having an enormous chest and shoulders, inhumanly long arms, and a small head with a dark face.

Fearing that the monster was after her children, Mrs. Chapman unfurled a blanket and used it as a screen to shield her little ones from the wildman's gaze. Ordering her children to stay behind her, she walked backwards from the cabin in the direction of the Fraser River. When they had put considerable distance between themselves and the giant, which had begun to examine the house, Jeannie and her children raced for the safety of Ruby Creek.

The Sasquatch Capital of Canada

Two hours later, George Chapman, none the wiser, returned home from work to find that his home had been ransacked. Specifically, he found that his storage shed had been broken into, and that a heavy barrel filled with dried fish had been hauled outside and torn open, apparently without the use of tools. George knew from the pair of 17-inch-long, humanlike footprints which encircled his cabin that the intruder had been a Sasquatch, one of the legendary wild men of the woods of which his people had long spoken. The tracks indicated that the giant had loitered about the home for some time before finally heading back into the mountains, tripping over a barbed wire fence as it departed the Chapmans' property.

To his relief, George quickly spied four smaller sets of human footprints leading along the Fraser River in the direction of Ruby Creek. He followed the tracks to his father's house, where he discovered his family had taken refuge.

Accompanied by George's father, who armed himself with a hunting rifle, the Chapmans returned to their cabin the following day. In the nights succeeding the incident, they heard strange howls emanating from the nearby woods. Sometimes they would awake in the morning to find huge footprints in the vicinity of the cabin. When the terrifying nocturnal visitations persisted for a week straight, the Chapmans decided to abandon their cabin and relocate.

In 1957, the Ruby Creek incident attracted the attention of John Willison Green, a Canadian journalist and one of Canada's most prominent Sasquatch researchers. Green was so impressed by the Chapmans' testimonies that he decided to settle in Harrison Hot Springs, where he lived and carried out his research until his death in 2016.

Frank Dean's Sighting

The incident at Ruby Creek, of course, was not the only Sasquatch sighting to take place around Harrison Hot Springs. Not by a long shot.

Back in March 1932, for example, several newspapers around Canada and the United States reported on an alleged sighting experienced by Frank Dean, a resident of Harrison Mills, located across the Harrison River from the Chehalis Reserve.

One night, the story goes, Dean was roused by the barking of his dog. He stepped outside to investigate the commotion and saw an enormous hairy man standing in the moonlight. The creature growled at Dean and began to advance towards him. Terrified, Dean stumbled back into his cabin and barred the door. The giant prowled about his cabin for some time before finally retreating into the bush.

Mrs. Caulfield's Experience

In the summer of 1934, the experience of a Mrs. James Caulfield, who lived with her husband on a farm outside Harrison Hot Springs, hit papers across the continent. While washing her clothes in the Harrison River, Mrs. Caulfield heard a noise similar to that of a hummingbird. In her own words:

"I turned my head but instead of a bird there stood the most terrible thing I ever saw in my life. I thought I'd die for the thing that made the funny noise was a big man covered with hair from head to foot. He was looking at me and I couldn't help looking at him. I guessed he was a Sasquatch so I covered my eyes with my hand, for the Indians say that if a Sasquatch catches your eye you are in his power. They hypnotize you. I felt faint and as I backed away to get to the house I tripped and fell. As he came nearer I screamed and fainted."

Fortunately, her scream attracted the attention of Mr. Caulfield, who ran to her assistance just in time to catch a glimpse of a huge hairy figure darting into the woods.

The Ruby Creek incident, Frank Dean's sighting, and Mrs. Caulfield's experience are but a few of the many Sasquatch stories to come out of Harrison Hot Spring. From peeking through windows at hapless farmwives to hurling rocks at Chehalis fishermen, the Sasquatch are said to have made fairly regular appearances in the Harrison area throughout the 1930s and '40s. Some say that the legendary wild man of the woods pays the occasional visit to his old stomping grounds to this very day.

Things to Do in Harrison Hot Springs

If, like J.W. Burns and John Green, you find yourself enthralled by the mystery of the Sasquatch, consider paying a visit to Canada's Sasquatch capital. There, you can hike the trails of Sasquatch Provincial Park- a natural area located about six kilometres (four miles) west of Ruby Creek- or brush up on your Sasquatch lore at the local Sasquatch Museum. A relaxing soak in Harrison's thermal waters makes for an excellent wind-down after a long day of Sasquatch hunting, and Sasquatch Days, with its canoe races and traditional salmon barbeque, offers a tantalizing glimpse into the culture of the Chehalis people, from whom the legend of the Sasquatch derives.

If you do decide to pay a visit to Harrison Hot Springs, remember to keep your eyes peeled. If you're really lucky, you might just catch a glimpse of the most famous forest-dwelling denizen of the Sasquatch Capital of Canada.

THE GIANT RIVER SNAKE OF SOUTHEAST ALBERTA

THE CITY OF MEDICINE HAT, nestled in the southeast corner of Alberta not far from the Saskatchewan border, has many claims to fame. Hockey fans know it as the home of the Medicine Hat Tigers, a ferocious junior hockey team which has produced NHL legends like Trevor Linden and Lanny McDonald. Road-trippers may associate Medicine Hat with its iconic Saamis Teepee- an enormous steel skeleton of a Plains Indian lodge which sits atop an old buffalo jump beside the Trans-Canada Highway. Of all its distinctive features, however, Medicine Hat is perhaps best known for its unusual name, which has its roots in a mysterious tangle of local native legends.

Medicine Hat was founded in 1883, when the Canadian Pacific Railway was built across the South Saskatchewan River. In the early 1900s, huge deposits of natural gas were discovered in the earth beneath it, prompting English writer Rudyard Kipling to famously remark that it boasted "all Hell for a basement". Its surfeit of natural gas, coupled with an abundance of red clay which lies along the banks of the South Saskatchewan River, transformed Medicine Hat into a major brick and ceramics manufacturing centre which once stood to compete with northwesterly Calgary for the distinction of being Alberta's most important city.

Despite a failed movement in the early 1900s to change its name to "Gasville" in an attempt to attract industry, Medicine Hat has retained its strange name since its founding. Its first citizens named the town after the old Indian name for the place, which, for a century prior to the town's founding, had served as a sort of boundary between the territories the Blackfoot Confederacy and that of their hereditary enemies, the easterly Plains Cree and Assiniboine.

There are a great number of old Blackfoot and Cree legends which purport to explain the origin of the name 'Medicine Hat', most of which local historian Marcel M.C. Dirk diligently documented in his 1993 book *But Names Will Never Hurt Me*. The majority of these legends are based on either a battle between the Blackfoot and the Cree, a love story involving human sacrifice, a landmark that looks like an Indian headdress, or some combination thereof. In spite of their differences, every single legend has something in common, namely the inclusion of a medicine man's headdress, or 'medicine hat'.

Giant River Snake of Southeast Alberta

James Sanderson's Story

In 1894, a Scots-Cree frontiersman-turned-rancher named James Sanderson, who was one of Medicine Hat's first citizens, documented a particular version of the 'medicine hat' legend in a series of articles for the *Medicine Hat News* entitled *Indian Tales of the Canadian Prairies*. Sanderson's tale is especially interesting as it constitutes one of the only recordings of an all-but-forgotten creature of Plains Indian oral tradition- an enormous supernatural river snake associated with the Great Spirit.

Sanderson began his tale by describing a certain setting on the South Saskatchewan River which is almost certainly the area between what is now Police Point Park and Strathcona Island Park, the former being opposite the river from the latter. At this particular point, the river bends substantially, resulting in a significant current which prevents the formation of ice "even during the most severe winters". At the centre of the bend is a small island, and to the east of the island are tall sandstone cutbanks, or cliffs, which fall into the river.

"This opening in the river is regarded with great interest by the Indians," Sanderson wrote, "as it is believed to be the breathing place of the Great Spirit who lives in the river and who, when he shows himself, assumes the form of a serpent..."

After laying out the setting, Sanderson proceeded to describe the legend:

"*Far back in Indian tradition, it is said that one of a hunting party of Blood Indians was sent forward to reconnoitre the country and see if the buffalo were to be met with any numbers. He was accompanied by his newly-married wife and a favourite dog, the latter bearing the travois- a crosspole arrangement to which the dog was harnessed- for the purpose of carrying some share of the travelling outfit.*

"*One evening, the Indian was camped by the river side and, as he was walking along near the opening in the river referred to, the serpent appeared to him and told him that if he would throw the flesh of his wife into the opening, he would become a great warrior and medicine man. The Indian returned to his tepee and repeated to his wife the words of the serpent. His wife at once expressed her willingness to die for the good of the tribe and in obedience to the call of the Great Spirit. Her husband, however, was reluctant and instead of his wife killed the dog. Carrying its carcass to the opening, he threw it in with the request that the Spirit might be pleased to accept from him his dog as a substitute for his wife. The Spirit refused to accept, and declared that, unless the Indian would sacrifice the wife he could do nothing for him. The man returned and informed his wife accordingly, and she again expressed her willingness to comply with the demand.*

"*Finally, she was sacrificed and her flesh given to the Spirit, who then directed the man to stay all night on the island near by, to rise early next morning, and, as the sun rose, to proceed towards the cutbanks lying to the east. At the base of one of the cutbanks he would find a bag containing medicines and a hat trimmed with ermine. He was instructed to bring back the medicine bag and the hat with him to the Spirit who would explain the purpose of the hat and the efficacy of the medicines. The hat, he was told, was to be worn only in war, and would ensure victory to the wearer. The tradition has it that the Indian became famous as a medicine man and warrior."*

How Seven Persons Got Its Name

Following the tale of the medicine hat, Sanderson documented another Indian legend featuring the Great Spirit in the form of a huge water serpent. This story takes place on Seven Persons Creek, a tributary of the South Saskatchewan which enters the river immediately adjacent to the island mentioned in the previous story. The tale purports to explain how the creek acquired its own strange name.

Before the coming of the North-West Mounted Police in 1874, the area of South Saskatchewan River and its tributaries in the vicinity of present-day Medicine Hat was a dangerous place frequented by raiding parties in search of trouble, and skirmishes and battles between Blackfoot and Cree warriors were common there. In 1872, a renowned war chief named Calf Shirt led a war party of Blood Blackfoot along Seven Persons Creek in search of enemies. Sanderson's tale describes an old Indian legend born of this particular excursion.

While crossing the creek a short distance above its confluence with the South Saskatchewan, the war party came across:

"... the dead bodies of seven men, lying just as if they had been suddenly struck down when following each other in Indian file. Although it was evident that they had been dead for some time, there was not a single indication of decay about them, unless the absence of any vestige of hair upon their heads might be regarded as such. They were not scalped; the hair had simply been removed without any indication being left of the manner of its removal. There was no wound visible on the bodies, nor could the Blackfoot tell whence they had come, or to what tribe they belonged.

"Being unable to explain this most mysterious find, the braves made up their minds to watch the bodies, to see whether anyone would come to claim them or give them burial. They waited patiently for five days in the neighbourhood and watched the corpses closely, but there was no sign of any such party appearing and the bodies continued in the same condition of non-decay.

"As they discussed various theories to account for the death of the men, someone suggested that they had died of starvation, but a close examination of their equipment proved that they had not been short of provisions. The final conclusion

of the Blackfoot was that the seven persons had, in some way, offended the Great Spirit who breathed through the unfreezing opening in the South Saskatchewan, and that he had punished then by striking them dead."

The natives reverently covered the bodies with stones which, for many years, remained undisturbed by prairie wolves and other scavengers, presumably remaining in their peculiar state of non-decay. Ever since, the waterway on which the bodies were discovered has been called Seven Persons Creek.

Earl Willows' Story

Intriguingly, Sanderson's tales are not the only documented Plains Indian legends involving giant supernatural water serpents. Blackfoot storyteller Earl Willows, for example, in a 2009 online article entitled "Earl Willows Tells the Story of the Warrior that Ate the Horned Snake", recounted a traditional Blackfoot tale in which two warriors, on their way home from a raid, accidentally set up camp over top of a snake den. In the morning, they discovered an enormous snake nearby and burned it alive. Heedless of his companion's warning, one of the warriors, named Weasel Calf, ate some of the snake's cooked meat which he plucked from the ashes.

The following morning, the other warrior, named Flint Knife, found that his companion had transformed into a massive horned snake. Weasel Calf asked his friend to bring his belongings back to his family, and urged him to maintain a healthy distance from him during their travels for his own safety. The two continued on until they came to a large river. Weasel Calf declared that this would be his new home, and asked Flint Knife to ask his family to come and visit him there.

Sometime later, the family of the metamorphosed brave visited the river and were greeted by the huge serpent who explained how his transformation came about. The snake then asked his family to leave, as he was afraid he would be unable to control his strange urge to harm them. The Blackfoot left the river and never returned.

The Horned Serpent

The Blackfoot and Cree legends of massive river snakes appear to be part of a much larger pan-American tradition of supernatural horned water serpents. From the Haida of the Pacific Northwest to the Mi'kmaq of the Maritimes, First Nations and Native American tribes across the continent all tell similar stories of powerful, often-horned water serpents imbued with supernatural abilities. For some reason, which this author hopes to investigate in a future article, these creatures are almost invariably considered the archenemies of Thunderbirds– legendary giant eagles which also enjoy a prominent place in indigenous folklore across North America.

Perhaps the most compelling pieces of evidence connecting the prairie legend of the giant water snake with this larger trans-continental tradition are the many striking similarities between Sanderson's 'medicine hat' story and a dark Ojibwa legend which appears in the 1859 book *Kitchi-gami: Wanderings Around Lake Superior*. *Kitchi-gami* is a travel memoir written by a German travel writer named Johann Georg Kohl, who spent the year 1855 living among the Ojibwa, voyageurs, and missionaries of Lake Superior. Near the end of his book, Kohl relates a local legend told to him by a Lake Superior native on the subject of the *'Matchi-Manitou'*– the evil spirit, whom the Ojibwa believe resides at the bottom of the water.

According to Kohl's informant, a local Indian once invoked the *Matchi-Manitou*, to the utter ruin of himself and his family. "When I inquired more closely how this all happened," Kohl wrote, "my *bonhomme* told me the following story:

"The man of whom he was speaking had once dreamed ten nights in succession that a voice spoke to him, saying that if he wished to have something very fine, which would make him happy, he must one night strike the water with a stick and sing a certain verse to it.

"He told this dream to his friends, who, however, dissuaded him, and said, 'Do not go, my friend- do not accept it.'

"On the eleventh night, when he dreamt the same thing again, he awoke his squaw, and said to her:

"'Dost thou not hear in the distance the drums clashing on the water? I must go there.' The squaw assured him, on the contrary, that she heard nothing; all was as quiet as mice. But he insisted that the drum could be heard quite plainly from the water, and he felt an irresistible call."

Heedless of his wife's exhortations to remain in the wigwam, the Indian rose from his furs and headed down to the lake shore. He produced a hefty stick, settled onto his haunches, and began beating the water's surface like a medicine man beats his drum, all the while singing the gloomy incantation he had learned in his dream.

"The water began gradually moving beneath the influence of his drumming," Kohl wrote, "and at last a small whirlpool was formed. He struck more rapidly, and his song grew quicker. The whirlpool became larger and more violent. The fish were at length drawn into it, and soon after them the other water animals. Frogs, toads, lizards, fish of every description, swamp and aquatic birds, with enormous swarms of swimming and flying insects, were drawn into the whirlpool, and passed snapping and quivering before the eyes of the enchanter, so that he nearly lost his senses."

As the whirlpool expanded, the water of the lake began to rise. Swallowing his horror, the Indian continued to sing the magic song and strike the roiling waters, his voice breaking into a shrill wail as the water crept higher, first past his waist, then above his shoulders, and further up his neck. Finally, in order to avoid drowning, the Indian fell silent.

"The waters calmed down," Kohl wrote, "the whirlpool and animals disappeared, the enchanter stood once more on the beach, and the water-king emerged from the placid lake, in the form of a mighty serpent."

The giant snake informed the Indian that he would make him healthy, rich, and prosperous in return for one of his children. When the Indian accepted the hideous offer, the serpent bowed his head, revealing a fiery, flower-like object nestled between its horns. With shaking hands, the native retrieved this item, which disintegrated into blood red powder in his palms.

The snake then informed the Indian that he was to collect twenty pieces of driftwood, each of which was to represent a particular desire. Whenever the Indian wished to satisfy a certain want, he would arrange the driftwood pieces in a semicircle around him on the beach, and then sprinkle some of the red powder on the piece representing the desire he wished fulfilled. Each time he did so, however, one of his children would become the property of the serpent.

"With these words," Kohl wrote, "the water-king disappeared into the depths. His adept... went home, where he found his squaw, who had watched all his doings with horror, already dead. Like her, the children were killed one after the other by the water-spirit. The wicked husband and father, who gave way to such bad dreams, was, for a long time, rich, powerful, and respected, a successful hunter, a much-feared warrior, and a terrible magician and prophet, until at length a melancholy fate befell him, and he ended his days in a very wretched manner."

GIANT WHITE WOLF SPOTTED IN NORTHERN SASKATCHEWAN

FOR AS LONG AS HUMAN beings have inhabited Canada's boreal forests, the wolf has occupied a place of special significance in the hearts and minds of subarctic Canadians. The native Dene peoples who pitched their moose hide teepees in the wilds of Northern Canada long before the white man made his appearance in that quarter believed that wolves were the reincarnated spirits of their ancestors, and often went to great lengths to avoid killing them. Many of those same Dene peoples, from the Han of central Yukon to the Slavey of the Northwest Territories, adopted the Wolf as the symbol of one of the two moieties into which they divided themselves, the other moiety usually being the Crow or the Raven; traditionally, a man of the Wolf moiety could only marry a woman of the Crow moiety, and *vice versa*. The Inuit who made their homes in the tundra north of Dene territory often trimmed the hoods of their parkas with wolf fur, since that substance, along with wolverine fur, is the only natural material on which humid breath will not depose into ice during wintertime. Even the white fur traders who began trickling into Northern Canada in the early 1800s, despite despising wolves for interfering with the trap lines of their native clients, often attempted to crossbreed their sled dogs with their wild subarctic cousins in the hopes of acquiring robust wolfdog puppies.

In addition to the domestic dog, Canada is currently home to twelve recognized subspecies of gray wolf, or 'timber wolf'. These subspecies can be roughly lumped into six categories based on their distribution and habitat: the Arctic Archipelago variety; the tundra and barrens variety; the Newfoundland and Labrador variety; the Pacific Northwest variety; the Great Lakes variety; and the northwestern forests variety. Although some biologists have argued that a few of these subspecies share too many similarities with each other to be classified as distinct, indigenous legend and frontier lore suggest that an additional variety of Canadian wolf ought to be added to the list.

For years, tales of a strange lupine monster currently unacknowledged by the scientific community have been leaking from Northern Canada to the Outside, as northerners often refer to southerly civilization. Since at least the 1950s, traders, trappers, and aboriginal Canadians have returned from the northern wilds with stories of an enormous solitary wolf said to haunt the boreal forests of Alaska, Yukon, and the Northwest Territories. Often referred to as the 'Waheela', this creature is typically described as having a wide head, a powerful build, a snow-white coat, and a size many times the magnitude of that of the average gray wolf.

I detailed a number of alleged Waheela sightings in my book *Legends of the Nahanni Valley*, and am pleased to present a new, never-before-published sighting here in this article. Experienced and brought to my attention by Justin Watkins of Spruce Lake, Saskatchewan, this sighting takes place at the southern edge of Canada's boreal forest, making it the southernmost Waheela sighting in recorded history, to the best of this author's knowledge.

Justin Watkins' Sighting

The following is Justin's own account of the sighting, lightly edited by this author for the sake of fluidity:

"A simple 7-Eleven trip turned into a horror I will never ever forget...

"It was the spring of 2011, and me and my friends were returning home from 7-Eleven, which was an hour away from Spruce Lake. My friend was driving a 1991 Ford Mustang, a fairly small car. The time was around 3:00 a.m., and we were flying- going speeds of up to 140 km/h (87 mph).

"We were about a kilometer from Spruce Lake when something in the ditch beside me caught my eye. It was a wolf. I

could barely make it out due to the darkness, but the headlight was shining a little into the ditch."

Incredibly, the creature kept pace with the vehicle, loping effortlessly with huge 7-foot-long strides, exhibiting the easy grace of a mountain lion and the steady persistence of a husky. Justin, incredulous, asked his friend to slow down. His buddy tapped on the brakes, and the vehicle decelerated to around 130 km/h (91 mph).

"When we slowed down, the wolf-like creature ran in front of the vehicle. Illumined by the headlights, we saw the whole thing. It was a sight I will never forget. The creature stood around 5 to 6 feet tall on all fours. It had a silverish white body, with huge teeth and a very wide head, and had fairly small ears. It dug into the highway as if it was nothing. I'd estimate the weight to be around four to five hundred pounds. It was outstanding. The beast was bigger than the car itself. The tail on it alone was almost half the size of the car.

"I'm a hunter. I've seen wolves, bears, and coyotes regularly throughout my whole life. What I saw that night was not a wolf..."

Fearing ridicule, Justin kept the extraordinary experience to himself until 2017, when an older man who struck up a conversation with him at the bar described seeing a similar animal himself many years prior. Instead of loping alongside his vehicle, however, the animal that this man encountered had chased after his truck.

Giant White Wolf of Saskatchewan

"There is something that lurks out here in these woods," Justin concluded, stating that American adventurer Frank Graves' Waheela encounter, as presented in this author's YouTube video *'Interview With a Cryptid Hunter'*, was what prompted him to come forward with his story. *"I still go out in the woods with another of my friends to look for it. It sounds unreal, but I will pass a lie detector test... The creature that I saw was something otherworldly. It feels reassuring to know that I am not alone in this adventure."*

What did Justin Watkins and his friends see on that fateful night in 2011? Could the enormous wolf they witnessed have been a relict Great Plains or Manitoba wolf- a member of the two large subspecies of gray wolf which once haunted the prairies of Central Saskatchewan before their supposed extinction a century ago? Could it have been a freakishly large Mackenzie Valley wolf plagued by gigantism? Was it some sort of prehistoric remnant, like a dire wolf or an *Amphicyon*, as some believe the Waheela to be? Was it a supernatural entity, a trick of the light, or a figment of the imagination? Or was it a specimen of another species entirely, which has yet to make its appearance in taxonomic literature? Whatever the case, Justin Watkins' testimony adds a tantalizing new piece to the ever-evolving puzzle of the Waheela- one of the greatest mysteries of Northern Canada.

TRAVERSPINE GORILLA: A WILDMAN FROM LABRADOR

THERE IS AN OLD tradition among the various Inuit tribes of Alaska, Northern Canada, and Greenland which holds that the North American Arctic was once home to a race of primitive giants called *Toonijuk*. Physically, these people were said to be immensely powerful, and could easily carry full-grown seals on their backs. They did not live in tents or igloos, like the Inuit, but rather in circular stone pit-houses roofed with whale ribs and animal skins.

Legend has it that, in ancient times, the Inuit began to hunt down the *Toonijuk* and greatly reduced their number. The giants who survived these predations fled to the mountains of the interior where, some say, their descendants still linger to this very day.

One area that has long been associated with the legend of the *Toonijuk* is the Torngat Mountain Range- a lonely, barren sierra in the tundra of the Labrador Peninsula

The Traverspine Gorilla

characterized by deep fjords and sheer rock faces. "Torngat" derives from an Inuktitut word meaning "place of spirits" which likely shares etymological ties with the name denoting the ancient, primitive giants of Inuit lore.

Another Labradorean locale connected with strange tales of wild giants is Happy Valley-Goose Bay, a Royal Canadian Air Force town located about 700 kilometres southeast of the Torngat Mountains, on the shores of Lake Melville and Grand River. In around 1913, a tiny settlement called Traverspine, located on the outskirts of this town, was the setting of several encounters with a mysterious creature which has come to be known as the Traverspine Gorilla.

The tale of the Traverspine Gorilla first appeared in print in American writer Elliot Merrick's 1933 book *True North: A Journey Into Unexplored Wilderness*. "Ghost stories are very real in this land of scattered, lonely homes and primitive fears," Merrick began.

According to Merrick, one autumn afternoon in around 1913, a little girl by the name of Michelin was playing alone in a meadow near Traverspine, not far from her parents' cabin, when she saw a strange manlike creature emerge from the woods. The thing was about seven feet tall, was covered in hair, and had long dangling arms, while its head was topped with a white mane that ran across the crown like the helmet crest of a Roman centurion. The creature grinned at the little girl, baring its white teeth, and beckoned for her to come closer. Miss Michelin screamed and raced for the safety of the house.

The creature left tracks all around the cabin and surrounding area. "It is a strange-looking foot," wrote Merrick, "about twelve inches long, narrow at the heel and forking at the front into two broad, round-ended toes. Sometimes its print was so deep it looked to weigh five hundred pounds."

Following Miss Michelin's terrifying encounter, local lumberjacks began to search for the creature. They set bear traps, of which the wily wildman steered clear, and lay in wait for it all night with their rifles at hand, to no avail. Although none were able to catch the creature, many observed its strange tracks in the dirt and snow. Others came across evidence indicating that the creature ripped bark off trees and uprooted huge logs as if in search of insects.

The wildman hung around the outskirts of Traverspine for two winters. It would often harass dogs, which barked and growled at it in the night, and would sometimes drive its canine contenders into the Traverspine River.

One afternoon, the creature made a second appearance at the Michelin home. One of the Michelin children noticed the creature peering into the cabin through a window and hollered for her mother. Mrs. Michelin stormed out of the house, shotgun in hand, just in time to see a white mane disappear into a clump of willows. She fired a shot at the

The Traverspine Gorilla

underbrush and heard a meaty thud which told her that her lead had found its mark.

According to Bruce S. Wright, one-time director of the Northeastern Wildlife Station of Fredericton's University of New Brunswick, who investigated the tale of the Traverspine Gorilla in June 1947, Mrs. Michelin said of her brush with the creature:

"It was no bear. I have killed twelve myself and I know their tracks well, and I saw enough of this thing to be sure of that. I fired a shotgun at it and heard the shot hit. My little girl was playing behind the house and she came running in saying it was chasing her. I grabbed the shotgun and went outside just in time to get a glimpse of it disappearing in the bush."

Wright, who documented the findings of his investigation in a letter to Canadian folklorist Philip Godsell, concluded his letter with the suggestion that the Traverspine Gorilla might be a barren ground grizzly, a rare subspecies of grizzly bear which roams the barrenlands of Nunavut and the Northwest Territories. He remarked that when he suggested this possibility to his Labradorean informants, "they all laughed at that as they were all very familiar with bear tracks."

Dr. C. Hogarth Forsyth, an English-American physician who operated a 20-bed hospital in the easterly community of Cartwright, Labrador, under the auspices of a charity called the Grenfell Association, shed some light on the strange footprints found in the Labrador wilderness from time to time in a newspaper interview conducted about six months prior to Wright's investigation. Forsyth described the tracks as "barefoot" and "ape-like", and claimed that they sometimes "led to nests under trees... Whatever made them climbed easily over stumps and other obstructions where ordinary man would have gone around." He stated that the tracks were certainly not bear tracks, as they were discovered and interpreted "by trappers whose living depends on their knowledge of tracks."

CRAWLER SIGHTING IN THE NORTHWEST TERRITORIES

EVERY YEAR, PEOPLE all over North America report encounters with strange creatures that have no place in current taxonomic literature. From sea serpents to Sasquatches, most of these mysterious animals have long featured in regional folklore. A small minority, like the Mothman of Point Pleasant, West Virginia, and the Manwolf of Elkhorn, Wisconsin, have no precedent at all.

In recent years, a new sort of monster sighting has emerged. These sightings are connected with a very special kind of mythology- one which far postdates the shadowy advent of native tradition and frontier lore. These monster myths derive from a unique variety of urban legend which has its origins in our burgeoning Age of the Internet- a fictional, viral horror story called the "creepypasta".

What are CreepyPastas?

Creepypastas are scary stories and images that proliferate across the internet to such an extent that they graduate into digital folklore. Instead of transmitting by way of playgrounds, after-school hangouts, and backyard campfires- the breeding grounds of traditional urban legends- these tales spread via chain emails, online forums like Reddit and 4Chan, and websites designed specifically for their dissemination.

Perhaps the most well-known creepypasta is the tale of Slenderman- a tall, thin, faceless, suit-clad gentleman who preys on children. The Slenderman character was invented on June 10, 2009, by a Japan-based American expat for an internet Photoshop contest. Images depicting this imaginary character and his associated backstory began to circulate throughout various online forums, and in no time the Slenderman meme went viral. Creative internet users began to expand on the Slenderman legend and formulate entire stories around him, transforming him into a full-blown 21st Century boogeyman.

In a 2012 interview for BBC Radio 4, Slenderman's creator, Eric Knudson, observed that "even though people [realize] that Slenderman was created [on an internet forum in] June 2009," some still believe that he might be real. Two years later, this strange reality made international headlines when two teenage girls from Wisconsin stabbed their friend half-to-death in the hope that their crime would earn them a home in Slenderman's supposed mansion in the woods.

The Rake

Slenderman is not the only creepypasta monster to escape from the internet and reify itself in the material world, or at least in the minds of imaginative internet users. Another virtual invention that makes its appearance from time to time is a creature known as "the Rake".

The Rake myth had its genesis in late 2005, when an anonymous poster on the imageboard website 4Chan decided to invent a new monster. The poster described his brainchild thus:

"Humanoid, about six feet tall when standing, but usually crouches and walks on all fours. It has very pale skin. The face is blank. As in, no nose, no mouth. However, it has three solid green eyes, one in the middle of its forehead, and the other two on either side of its head, towards the back... When it attacks, a mouth opens up, as if a hinged skull that opens at the chin. Reveals many tiny, but dull teeth".

This monster, which appears to have been inspired by the so-called "Crawlers" from the 2005 horror film *The Descent*, evolved throughout the 4Chan thread, gradually transforming into a gaunt, naked, pale-skinned, human-like creature that crawls on four long spindly limbs. This entity was dubbed 'the Rake'.

It would be several years before the concept of the Rake gained traction in the creepypasta community. In December 2008, posts featuring this made-up monster appeared on the Russian social networking site LiveJournal. In April 2009, the creature returned to 4Chan, its birthplace. Two months later, the Rake made its way onto SomethingAwful.com, where it served as an inspiration for Eric Knudson's Slenderman.

By 2010, the legend of the Rake was spreading like wildfire throughout the internet, infiltrating all manner of creepypasta websites and engendering fan art and creative fiction which added depth and colour to its mythos.

Crawler Sightings

Then, in 2012, something incredible happened: internet users, ostensibly in earnest, began reporting frightening encounters with emaciated, pale, hairless, man-like creatures that crawled on all fours. Apparently oblivious to the fact that the objects of these encounters bore striking resemblance to the fictional Rake, internet users attempted to equate these entities with characters of Native American mythology. Some suggested that they were skinwalkers- medicine men of Navajo lore who possess the ability to transform into animals. Others proposed that these bony humanoids were manifestations of the Wendigo- an evil cannibalistic spirit of Cree and Algonquin legend. Others still began to invent new names for these creatures, such as "fleshgaits", "goatmen", and "crawlers", the latter evoking the 2005 movie villains who likely helped to inspire the Rake in the first place.

It would be tempting to dismiss these sightings as attention-seeking hoaxes or innocent misidentifications owing to the power of suggestion were it not for their chilling profusion. The staggering quantity of reliable witnesses who claim to have seen these creatures, coupled with the fact that many witnesses appear to be ignorant of the urban legend which their sightings evoke, suggests two almost inconceivable possibilities: that the creator of the Rake meme, through some mysterious process, unconsciously contrived an entity that already existed, or that the human imagination somehow willed these beings into existence. These bizarre notions beget the uncomfortable question: "What came first: the monster or the myth?"

Don Herbert's Sighting

In January 2019, a northern Canadian named Don Herbert shared his own crawler sighting with this author. Herbert is a miner who hails from the remote town of Hay River, Northwest Territories, located on the southern shores of Great Slave Lake. He works in biweekly rotations, spending two weeks at the mine followed by two weeks off at home.

One night in mid-August 2018, during his annual summer vacation about a week prior to his scheduled return to work, Herbert found himself alone in his truck, driving through the woods on the Northwest Territories Highway 2, more commonly known as the Hay River Highway. This stretch of road is one of the most remote thoroughfares in all of Canada, beginning on the shores of Great Slave Lake and skirting the western bank of the Hay River before joining the Mackenzie Highway 38 kilometres to the south.

Drowsy, road-weary, and anxious to get home, Don was a few miles from town when a pale figure appeared in his truck's headlights, crouching on all fours in the ditch on the left-hand side of the road. From wolves to wolverines, Don had encountered plenty of animals during nighttime drives through the boreal wilderness, but this creature was unlike anything he had ever seen before. Its skin was grayish white and completely hairless. Its head, which he estimated to be only slightly smaller than his own, was bald and didn't appear to have any ears. Aside from a pair of dark eyes, its only facial feature was a cruel-looking, beak-like mouth. Its legs were long and spindly, and appeared to taper sharply towards the feet, which were obscured by long grass.

The creature, which impressed Don as being highly intelligent, appeared to notice him in the driver's seat. Bearing its beaklike teeth, it crouched slightly, dug in with its front legs, and launched itself at Don's truck, leaving a small cloud of dust in its wake. Instead of slamming into the side of the vehicle as its course indicated it was likely to, the creature turned deftly on the side of the road and loped alongside the truck.

Alarmed, Don stepped on the gas and raced for home, leaving the frightening creature behind in the gloom of the forest.

In the months that followed his horrifying encounter, Don spent his free time attempting to identify and track down the strange animal that he saw, secretly fearing that it was a demon. The following is Don Herbert's own account of his search for the mysterious crawler, lightly edited by this author for the purposes of concision and continuity, which he has generously allowed me to publish for the first time in this article.

Don Herbert's Account

"During that remaining week, I did not return to the location of the encounter with the creature. More specifically, I could not return to the location. I was now absolutely terrified to do so. Even in daylight, not a chance.

"Around this time, things were starting to sink in and I started to notice some fundamental changes starting to happen with my behavior.

"I reside in town, and my house faces the Hay River. The house itself is set back a ways from the street, resulting in a fairly long driveway of maybe 30 feet or so. I can walk across the street in front of my home and access a nature trail that follows the river. On the other side of the river is wilderness,

save for a gravel road that provides access to a First Nations reserve. Directly behind my home there is a green area as well.

"A couple of days after the incident, I was taking my garbage to the curb after dark. There is a streetlamp across the street so it wasn't entirely pitch black. However, as I was carrying my garbage can to the curb, I felt a sense of nervousness starting to develop. It became worse the closer I got to the woods on the opposite side of the street at the end of the driveway.

"As I progressed to the street, I couldn't help but to continue to scan the tree line on the opposite side of the road in both directions, watching for any signs of movement. After I placed my garbage can at the street, I could not bring myself to turn my back to the darkened woods out of a deep sense of fear.

"To return to the house, I back stepped the length of the driveway, keeping a close eye on the tree line until I reached the front end of my truck, which was parked in the driveway. Only then did I turn around to make the final distance onto my front deck, then into my house with my back to the woods. I knew then and there that the encounter with the creature had affected me more than I cared to admit.

"Up until that point, I was trying my hardest to put the incident out of my mind and continue on as normal. I did not want to even start thinking about it. Every time my thoughts wandered back to it, I would try thinking of something else entirely. I didn't even want to begin to try and form an opinion. I was hoping I could just forget about the encounter altogether

and just simply move on. Well, let's just say that's easier said than done.

"When I got back into my house after putting the trash out, I sat down on the couch. I realized at that moment in time that there was no way that I was going to be able to avoid confronting the subject. The simple fact of the matter was, those 4 to 5 seconds on the highway that night had changed my life forever, whether I tried to continue to deny it to myself or not.

"And so it began. I asked myself the one question I was trying my absolute best to avoid from the very moment I passed by the creature and the encounter ended: 'What in the hell was that?'

Research

"I returned to work for my two-week rotation shortly after that.

"I started to tell the story to as many people as I could in the hopes that someone may have had a similar story or shared a similar experience. I wondered if I'd had a hallucination. I surfed the web for images similar to creature I had seen. I read reports of sightings of strange creatures in the hope that someone out there may have experienced a similar encounter. I was sincerely hoping to find a natural explanation for what I had seen.

"When I started looking for information on the creature, there were only two options at this point that I really cared to entertain:

"The first, and most probable, in my mind, was that I had experienced a hallucination of some sort. What confused me most about this theory was that I had not only seen the creature, but I had heard it as well. The experience just seemed too real.

"The second option was that I had perhaps witnessed a species of animal never before seen or reported. This is where I was 'officially' introduced to the world of cryptozoology. Now don't get me wrong, I was not totally ignorant of the cryptid world prior to this encounter. In fact I probably possess more knowledge about the subject than most average people.

"I currently prospect the Nahanni region, and earlier in life spent two seasons placer mining on the Liard River just a ways upriver from its confluence with the South Nahanni. You can't research the area from a geological perspective in a search for minerals or frequent the region without becoming aware of the mysteries surrounding the area. I have always tried to keep an open mind about things, but the moment of my encounter was the first time I actually thought that some of the stories I've read and some of tales I've heard over the years could potentially have some measure of truth to them."

Frustrated by his inability to identify the creature, the incredulity of his co-workers, and his newfound fear of the wilderness which infringed upon his lifelong love of outdoor recreation, Don resolved to find the creature and kill it.

The Tracks

"I returned from work on the evening of September 4th, 2018, arriving home at just after 8:00 PM. As we were landing at the airport, the sun was just starting to dip below the horizon.

"Tim, a friend I work with, who was also on the flight, kindly offered me a lift home from the airport. Tim was the first person to whom I had relayed the story of my encounter. I had been very anxious to speak with him two weeks earlier, as I waited for the flight to the mine. In the past, Tim has both hunted and trapped to make a living. He has extensive knowledge of the subject. I thought that if anyone would have seen or heard of anything like this creature, it would be him.

"When Tim dropped me off at home, he was then heading to his own home and family. They reside on an acreage about 10 minutes south of town in the direction of where I saw the creature. Tim's family also owns a secluded cottage along the Hay River near the Alberta / NWT border, and as such they spend a lot of time on the highway travelling back and forth, passing the location where I had seen the creature.

"Tim knew I intended to try to find the track that evening and wished me luck. When he dropped me off at home, I quite literally tossed my bags inside the door of my home, got in my truck, and proceeded to head out on the highway to where the encounter with the creature had taken place.

"At this point in time, the encounter was all I could think about. It was very quickly becoming an obsession, if indeed it hadn't already. Before I could even begin to move forward I had to find the answer to one fundamental question: 'Did it leave any tracks?' Visions and spirits and hallucinations do not leave physical tracks.

"Three weeks had now elapsed since the encounter. I didn't feel I had much chance of success in finding any tracks in the ditch where I first noticed the creature or on the shoulder of the highway where it approached me, as it had rained a few times in the two weeks I was at work. I was hoping beyond hope that I was not already too late.

"Even with the sun now below the horizon and darkness fast approaching, I had to go. I could not take the chance of one more minute of time elapsing before I had the opportunity to find that sign. I felt my very sanity now hinged on finding that one, single, particular track on the shoulder of the highway. This was not only a search for a strange creature but also an attempt to confirm that I wasn't on the path of early dementia or beginning to lose grip on reality.

"On the drive out, I was trying to reconcile the fact that this could go two ways. The first was that, if I found the tracks, it would mean the creature is real. The second was that, if I didn't find the tracks, it would mean that I'm losing my mind.

Crawler Sighting in NWT

Neither option was very appealing. It was not the most pleasant drive, to say the least.

"*I slowed as I approached the area the encounter took place and there it was- the skid mark the creature had left, just where I thought it would be. I parked on the side of the road about 20 feet from the track. I got out with my iPhone on record to get some video I could look at later. I was not stepping one foot off the pavement, however. I scanned the area with my phone as long as I dared and got the hell back in the truck and started heading back to town.*

"*I had to get Tim!!! I had to get Tim!!! I had to get Tim!!!*

"*That was all I could think as I drove back to Tim's place 10 minutes away, hoping that I could get him to take a look at the track before dark. I could not stop myself from imposing on Tim, who had just returned to his family after two weeks. I just had to get Tim!*

"*Tim was gracious enough to come out with me and examine the track. He offered his opinion that it looked similar to a goat track, but since the track was at least three weeks old, you would never be able to tell for sure. This would be unusual, as goats aren't known in the region.*

"*As Tim was now with me, I managed to summon the courage to now actually step off the pavement and have a look in the ditch where I first spotted the creature. In the dim light, I could tell something had left signs of activity. But the signs were* only faintly visible due to their age. I also followed the path it took up the ditch towards the gravel shoulder and found its approach tracks as well.

"We didn't spend a great deal of time investigating the tracks due to the failing light and soon headed back home.

"It was dark as I dropped Tim back off at home. The tree line across from my driveway was dark as I returned home to the couch. I had some thoughts to process and a heart to get back in my chest.

"While having my coffee the next morning I decided to try out a new hobby and become an amateur cryptozoologist (LOL). I intended to approach the hunt for the creature in a scientific manner the best I could and let the experts come to their own conclusions based on any evidence I could gather.

"Finding the track made me confident that I was dealing with an animal. My former anger subsided into fascination. I decided to set out to prove that this thing exists."

Don Herbert began his investigation at an abandoned gravel pit located about a mile from the site of his encounter. The area was perpetually crisscrossed with animal tracks, and Don hoped that the mysterious creature might leave some sign of its presence there. For nearly two weeks, he checked the site every morning for fresh prints. On the twelfth day, his diligence was rewarded; there, in the frost-encrusted soil, were two pairs of strange animal tracks which he interpreted as belonging to a mother and her offspring. Herbert reasoned that the presence of a young one might explain the creature's hostile reaction on the highway; perhaps the creature had been attempting to chase him off, or direct his attention away from her progeny.

Herbert proceeded to search for the creatures' den in the woods near the site of his encounter, on the side of the highway closest to the river, reasoning that the creature's hairlessness was an indication that it hibernated during the winter. During his search, he came across several more of the strange prints. These tracks often appeared in the vicinity of wolf tracks, which Don took as an indication that the creature is a scavenger which subsists on the leavings of predators.

On September 17, 2018, Don Herbert discovered the outlet of an old drainage culvert which was covered with fresh vegetation, as if someone or something had attempted to conceal it. He suspected that this might be the creatures' den, and set up game cameras to monitor the entrance. When the cameras failed to yield any interesting footage, Don crawled into the culvert and found it empty and unusually clean.

Identifying the Tracks

Don Herbert took several photos of the strange animal's tracks during his investigation and showed four of the best of them to experienced animal trackers with whom he was personally acquainted. None of the woodsmen were able to identify the tracks. He then sent the photos to the Alliance of

Mysteries of Canada: Volume II

Natural History Museums of Canada. The Alliance forwarded the photos to several biologists, none of whom were able or willing to interpret them.

The Mystery Creature's Tracks

This author of this piece later sent Don's photos to two expert animal trackers, one of them a distinguished Canadian hunter who preferred to remain anonymous. Both experts claimed that the tracks in three of the photos were too faint to accurately identify, but agreed that the track featured in Figure 3 is clearly that of a wolf.

After doing a little research of his own, this author, who is admittedly a complete novice when it comes to interpreting animal tracks, observed that the tracks in Figures 1 and 2 appear to bear some resemblance to the prints left by wolverines.

Mysteries of Canada: Volume II

The Creepypasta Connection

When asked to produce a sketch of the mysterious animal he saw, Don sent this author an illustration made by DeviantArt artist DemonGirl99, which he claimed was very similar to the creature he witnessed.

Crawler Sighting in NWT

In private correspondence with this author, DemonGirl99 claimed that her illustration was based off another image produced by fellow DeviantArt creator Crypdidical. This original piece features the "Fisherman"- a Rake-like monster which Crypdidical invented. In an accompanying description, the artist explained his creation thus:

"Much like The Slender Man and the Tall Gentleman, the Fisherman is a mysterious humanoid entity which seems bent on creating terror and fear in [its] wake... It has only been seen around water, and often shows itself to small groups or individuals of its choosing.

["Its] figure has never been glimpsed in full light. But from what can be understood from witnesses that come across it... it is extremely lanky. It often walks on four limbs, and never on two. It's agile and coordinated, and seems to be able to guide [its] long [appendages] with ease and grace..."

Mysteries of Canada: Volume II

The Trail Camera Photos

Don Herbert assured this author that he fully intended to continue the search for the mysterious creature, which he believed to be an undiscovered species of terrestrial origin, and agreed to furnish me with any updates on his progress.

In November 2019, nine months after his previous correspondence, Herbert got in touch with this author a second time, claiming to have finally photographed the creature with trail cameras he had set up for that purpose. Attached to his message was a startling nighttime photograph of hibernal taiga, in the left background of which, in the shadows of the forest, crouched a pale, black-eyed, malevolent-looking creature identical in appearance to the mysterious roadside monster described by Herbert.

Crawler Sighting in NWT

The excitement which this tantalizing new development engendered in this author was tempered somewhat by one of Herbert's follow-up photographs, which depicted the same patch of boreal forest in the summertime and in daylight, its features unobscured by snow and darkness. In this second photo, in the same spot at which the creature lurked in the winter photo, sits a tangle of branches. In this author's opinion, at least, this snarled foliage bears vague resemblance, in both shape and dimension, to the sinister-looking figure from the winter photo, hinting at the possibility that the disturbing form constitutes little more than a cluster of scrub covered with snow, its frightening appearance merely the result of pareidolia- the human tendency to perceive human-like features in random patterns and formations.

Then again, Herbert's trail cameras only take photos in response to movement. *Something* caused the shutter to open on the night the picture was taken. Was it a feather or a fragment of greenery blown by an errant gust of wind? The night appears to have been calm and still, judging from the state of the trees. Had a squirrel or an owl skittered into the frame? No such animals appear in the photo. Or could the camera truly have responded to the motion of the same spooky creature witnessed by Don Herbert on the side of the Hay River Highway, crawling its way through the snow?

Newfoundland - 2010

Intriguingly, Don Herbert is not the only Canuck to report an encounter with a crawler in the Canadian backwoods. In 2012, a Reddit user with the handle "TossO" described his own brush with a similar creature in an unidentified national park in Newfoundland in the summer of 2010.

While cruising through a barren valley one moonlit night, the poster saw a large, stocky, naked, humanoid creature crawling rapidly towards a stretch of road that lay before him. The creature was completely hairless, and its skin was "a deathly, nauseating white with a greasy shine".

As he approached the creature, the poster observed that "it had a rubbery face, distorted by hate or a scream, [and] black eyes that reflected in the moonlight". The poster was horrified by the creature's facial expression, which gave him the impression that "it was intelligent, and . . . wanted to tear [him] apart with its teeth".

Similar to Don Herbert's creature, this monster appeared to be on a collision course with the poster's vehicle. "I braced for it to run into my car door," the Redditor wrote. "And then it was gone. The [rear-view] mirror showed me nothing."

TossO ended his post by voicing his suspicion, evocative of one of Don Herbert's theories, that the creature he witnessed was a demon.

Northern Ontario - 1990s

In 2017, Reddit user Bailbondshman claimed to have encountered an emaciated, human-like figure while on a camping trip with his father somewhere in Northern Ontario's cabin country when he was nine or ten years old. While canoeing on a lake with his father during a mussel-hunting excursion, the Redditor caught a glimpse of something strange amidst the trees on the shore.

"I couldn't make it [out] very well," the Redditor wrote, "but it was white, almost like the texture of birch, and very lankly. I remember thinking that... it definitely wasn't a person, but it wasn't too far from the general shape of one. It was staggering around lethargically and slowly; if it was an animal, then something was definitely wrong with it. I waded over to my dad and told him to look up there, and by that point it was gone..."

Later on in the post, the Redditor related other interesting (if unrelated) anecdotes regarding this particular camping spot, including one involving a strange humming noise that he and his father would sometimes hear in the nearby marshes, which was often preceded by sudden and utter silence, and another revolving around a small peninsula on the lake that was covered with mushrooms and dead trees and pervaded by a terrible stench.

The Redditor ended his post with what he considered the most disturbing story regarding the lake on which he and his father would often vacation:

"I remember one morning, I had woken up just before sunrise and was still in bed. In the window adjacent to my bed, I saw something that usually wasn't there. It was half a . . . face poking around the edge of the window and staring into our cabin. Sickly pale orange with giant black holes where the eyes were supposed to be. This thing was definitely not human. I... hid under the covers, and eventually fell back to sleep. When I woke up again, everyone was also awake, and there was no sign of anything there."

The Ovens Natural Park, Nova Scotia - 2015

Crawlers are not the only creepypasta-esque creatures purported to wander the Canadian wilderness. In recent years, several Reddit users claimed to have witnessed tall, thin, naked, bipedal humanoids, bearing characteristics of both Slenderman and the Rake, in various Canadian locales. One of these is Redditor LilyBirdGk, who created a post in 2016 in which she described her boyfriend's strange encounter with a mysterious entity the previous summer.

In August 2015, the poster and her boyfriend rented a cabin in The Ovens Natural Park, Nova Scotia- an area famous for its spectacular seaside cliffs and their many sea caves, or "ovens". They spent their first day in the park hiking a cliffside trail and exploring the area's eponymous formations.

That night, the couple and a few of their friends settled down in their rented cabin for a game of cards. The poster's boyfriend lost gracelessly, his temper exacerbated by jokes directed at him by one of his friends, which were intended to poke fun at his stature. To cool off, he decided to go for a walk outside alone.

When her boyfriend failed to return after half an hour, the anxious poster called him on his cellphone. He did not answer her call, but quickly phoned her back and asked where she was. The poster, somewhat confused, replied that she was still in the cabin. After a pause, the boyfriend declared that he was coming back immediately, his voice betraying a hint of alarm. When he finally arrived at the cabin, he told his girlfriend a disturbing tale:

"He had walked out to the trails to get some fresh air and sat down on one of the benches to look out at the ocean. The moon was pretty bright that night so everything was illuminated pretty well. Then he heard someone walking by and he saw this really tall and pale figure stop and look at him, and then continue on. For some reason he assumed this was me coming to look for him, and [that's] when I called him and told him I was in the cabin. He said that in retrospect it was inhumanly tall and pale (thanks babe) and [couldn't] possibly be a person. He was not himself for the rest of the night and [didn't] seem normal until lunch the next day."

Quesnel, British Columbia - 2018

Throughout the latter half of 2018, Reddit user MZULFT10989 posted about his own encounters with a strange entity which visited his property in the city of Quesnel, in central British Columbia.

The Redditor's first alleged encounter took place in the early summer, when he noticed an eerie humanoid creature "running inhumanly fast" through the field behind his house before vaulting over a 5.5-foot-tall fence and disappearing into the woods. This creature was emaciated, white-skinned, and "at least 7 feet tall", with a gaping mouth and no eyes. Unlike the crawler that Don Herbert encountered, this creature was bipedal, and ran with a manlike gait.

In August 2018, the same Redditor published another post in which he claimed to have seen the mysterious creature again, this time at night, darting through a field on his property and jumping the fence into his neighbour's yard. Two weeks later, the Redditor caught the same creature peering at him from around the side of his house. Frightened, he retreated indoors. Later, he examined the area at which the creature had stood and found scratch marks on the exterior of his house.

In October 2018, the Redditor reported a third encounter. While he was sitting outside on the back porch facing his field, the creature appeared and raced across his property as it had done several times before. This time, however, it stopped in the middle of the field and turned to stare at the Redditor. Before the petrified Canadian had time to react, the creature ran down the field and leapt into his neighbour's yard.

On another occasion, the poster saw the creature peering at him through his living room window. He ran upstairs to retrieve his hunting bow, with which he intended to protect himself, but by the time he returned downstairs, the creature was gone.

The subject of the Redditor's fourth and final post took place in November 2018, about two weeks after his previous encounter. This time, the man found the creature staring into his barn through an open window. The entity apparently learned that it was being watched, turned to face the Redditor, and emitted a piercing shriek before running into his neighbour's yard and into the woods.

Missy Sterling's Encounter

Although it's not exactly a Canadian crawler story, the author of this book has decided to end this chapter with a lightly-edited transcript of an audio clip sent to him by a lovely lady from the southern United States named Missy Sterling. Several years ago, Sterling had her own encounter with a strange, pale, humanoid creature on a highway in Alabama. Her experience has several interesting congruencies with that told by Don Herbert, of which she was unaware at the time. Specifically, both Missy and Don encountered their creatures while driving, both subsequently struggled to rationalize the event in their minds, and both, in the aftermath of their encounters, developed fears regarding their sanity.

Sterling described her encounter to this author in the audio clip thus:

Crawler Sighting in NWT

"It's been a couple of years since my experience. I was on my way home from my mother's house. She lives in Vernon, Alabama, and I live in Columbus, Mississippi, right on the state line. So, I'm driving on the road, and up ahead I can see something in the road. At first, I think it's a deer- these roads are heavily populated in the wintertime with deer, and in the summer too; there's deer everywhere.

"So I start slowing down and, by the time I reach this thing, I'm at a complete stop. And I'm looking at it, and I'll be completely honest: I pissed myself, because this was like nothing I had ever seen before. I had this experience where my brain was running patterns and coming up with nothing. This thing... it looked like it was a baby. It was smaller, and I don't know where I got this sense from, but I felt like it was a kid. Not a human kid, though, because this thing was a weird, weird white colour. It was chalk white. It had these huge eyes, and it reflected my headlights, but they were black. It had a slit for a mouth, and it looked terrified.

"I got the sense that it was just as scared as I was, and it was frozen, kind of like a deer in the headlights. I was, too; for a second I froze. I don't know how long I was just sitting there in the middle of the road, just stopped with this thing in front of my vehicle.

"When I came upon it, it was on all fours, and then it stood up on two legs and walked off. Its movements were very jerky, like nothing I'd ever seen. And it let out this screech... ooh, I'm getting chills right now.

"I just noped the hell out of there. I felt like I was scrambled, I couldn't get myself together, and so I got off the road, and I pulled over, and I cried.

"I had to go home and change my pants. I got home, and I didn't say anything at first because... you wonder if you're crazy, if you hallucinated. You try to do anything to rationalize the experience, because it is completely irrational. Then I started telling people about it. I was surprised that no one really made fun of me. They were a bit freaked out, but I hadn't found anyone who had experienced anything similar.

"Some time goes by, and I can't let it go. I started looking online, and I came across this video completely by accident. This guy called Richard Grebenik, he filmed this thing in his backyard, through his porch screen. When I saw the video, chills ran down my spine, because the movements, the whiteness... it was unmistakable. The video comments are full of people saying, "Oh, this is fake" and "There's a naked crackhead in your yard". But you can hear this guy on the phone with his preacher- he called his preacher- and he is just freaked out. He asked the preacher to start praying, and the guy does. You can tell he's very obviously freaked out. But more than anything, the movement of this thing is what made me believe it was a 100% authentic video. I don't see how someone could re-create that...

Crawler Sighting in NWT

"There's another video from Canada, actually, of some white creature stalking a moose on the roadside. Everybody says, "Oh, it's a smudge on the window". I don't see how anyone could say that. It made the same jerky movements as the thing that I saw.

"I don't know what the thing is, but there's definitely something to it."

KELLY CHAMANDY: CANADA'S LAST BEAR OIL SALESMAN

I F YOU'RE A FAN OF Westerns, chances are that you're familiar with the snake oil salesman- the slick confidence man who rides into town with a cart filled with worthless patent medicines, falsely accredits his potions with curative properties, sells his wares to a handful of gullible customers, and hits the trail before his deception can be found out. This character derives from actual 19th Century American quack doctors who passed bottles of mineral oil off as genuine snake oil- a traditional Chinese medicine.

A while back, my friend, Kevin Guhl, while working on a fascinating research project that will knock the socks off the Fortean community, came across the tale of Kelly Chamandy, Canada's most famous bear oil salesman. Chamandy was a 20th Century woodsman from northern Ontario who garnered international renown for selling bottles of black bear grease to balding men and women, alleging that his ursine pomade helped to reverse hair loss. Quite unjustly,

I was quick to categorize him as a sort of Canadian snake oil salesman- an unscrupulous businessman who preyed on people's hopes and fears in the pursuit of profit. A closer look at this most colourful of characters, however, reveals another picture entirely.

Early Life

Kelly Chamandy was born in 1902 in the city of North Bay, Ontario, on the northern shores of Lake Nipissing. His father, A.K. Chamandy, was a Syrian peddler who named his son after his friend and neighbour, an Irishman who had treated him and his wife kindly upon their immigration to Canada.

When he was still a young boy, Kelly's family moved 370 kilometres north to the town of Cochrane, Ontario, where his father opened his first store. There, at the age of six, while riding in a packsack on the back of a Cree Indian, he saw his first black bear- an animal around which his life would come to revolve.

The Fur Trade

When he came of age, Kelly headed to the woods of Northern Ontario and became a fur trader. His subsequent adventures formed the basis of many a tale, both tall and true, to which he would often treat visitors to his store.

One of these stories involved an incident that took place during a bear hunt, which Kelly undertook with a fellow fur trader and several Inuit friends in James Bay (the southern appendage of Hudson Bay). This was no mere black bear hunt, Kelly was quick to assure his audience. "Hunting blacks is a pushover," he would say. "It is the polars and grizzlies which are a man's job."

On this hunting trip, while boating along the coast of North Twin Island (a large isle in the middle of James Bay), Kelly and his companions saw a huge polar bear with her cub walking along the shore. Brandishing spears, the Inuit disembarked with three of their dogs and prepared to hunt the mother bear the traditional way.

"A polar bear always lunges to the left," Kelly told Don Deleplante, a writer for *Maclean's* magazine who interviewed him in the early 1950s. "The Eskimos timed their thrusts for this movement which they knew would occur... The bear seemed to be on one man, then another, but always the dogs leaped in in time. The courage of the little men before the white monster was fantastic."

One of the hunters finally managed to kill the bear by planting the butt of his spear into the ground and swinging the business end towards the bear as it barreled towards him. "The bear impaled itself on a blade two and a half feet long and smashed the haft with the force of the charge. The sons ran after the cub and killed it. The three laughed like madmen."

Another tale with which Kelly would often regale tourists was the story of a wrestling match that he claimed to have won against a bear during a springtime business trip to a Cree village. While attempting to cross a steam, he leapt from a high rock to a ledge on the bank. Upon landing, he found himself sharing the ledge with an enormous grizzly which had been looming over the water with its paw extended, attempting to catch fish. The ledge was too high to jump from, and the bear was blocking the only exit. When Kelly cautiously approached the animal, it lunged at him.

For about thirty seconds, Kelly Chamandy- a burly, bearlike man himself, with broad shoulders and thick, muscular arms- grappled with the monster. Finally, he pressed his back against the rock wall behind him and delivered a two-footed kick to the bear's belly, sending the bruin behemoth crashing into the stream below.

"Say," Chamandy would say at the end of his incredible tale, "don't believe that story about the bear fishing by standing watch over a stream and knocking the fish from the water by a sweep of its paw. A bear dives right in to get fish."

Kelly Chamandy eventually established an independent fur trading post in the town of Moosonee, Ontario, about twelve miles up the Moose River from James Bay. There, in the late 1930s, he met a tall, grey-eyed woman named Frances Violet Pullen. Ten years his junior, Frances was the daughter of a local railway foreman. Kelly courted and married Frances, and a year later, the couple had their first child- a son named Monty.

Misfortune and Disaster

About a month after Monty's birth, Kelly Chamandy reported on the dramatic rescue of a 15-man French-Canadian survey team, the members of which nearly starved to death in the frozen muskeg country of Northern Quebec, having failed to find the food cache that had been prepared for them on account of heavy snowfall. Chamandy interviewed 32-year-old Leo Bernier, the most emaciated of the crew, while he lay on a bed in a Moosonee inn. Bernier's account, which Kelly translated from French to English, was published in the January 3, 1938 issue of the *Ottawa Evening Citizen*.

A year and a half later, Kelly Chamandy had his own brush with disaster. In early July, 1939, Kelly, his wife Frances, and their 17-month-old son Monty- along with four Cree employees named Tom Linklater, Willie Isserhoff, John Wesley, and Alec Simion- set out on a fur-buying trip. They piled into the *Kittiwake*, a 40-foot-long fishing boat which Kelly had purchased shortly after his wedding, and headed down the Moose River into James Bay, bound for the Cree village of Attawapiskat. While they were on the water, a ferocious gale blew in from the north and inflicted serious damage upon Chamandy's vessel. The crew was forced to abandon the craft and row for shore in a canoe. Although the seven passengers safely made landfall at a place called

Partridge Creek, the *Kittiwake* was wrecked beyond repair, bringing $35,000-worth of Kelly Chamandy's trade goods with it to the bottom of James Bay.

Six months later, Chamandy was hit with another misfortune: his family's cabin at Moosonee mysteriously burned to the ground. By that time, war had broken out in Europe, and in order to both support his family (which would soon gain another member, baby Ulna) and serve his country, Kelly Chamandy enlisted in the Royal Canadian Air Force.

When he finally came home for good at the end of the war, Kelly Chamandy was bald as an egg. Taking the advice of his Cree friends, he began massaging rendered bear fat into his scalp and, lo and behold, his hair began to grow back! The state of his pate, his Syrian peddler heritage, and his wilderness experience gave him a brilliant idea which led to his entrance into an ancient, unconventional, and all-but-forgotten industry: the bear grease market.

Kelly Chamandy's Bear Grease

From the mid-1600s until the end of the 19th Century, many wealthy Europeans anointed their scalps and greased their whiskers with the rendered fat of Russian brown bears, hoping that the tallow contained the same mysterious property which gave bears their thick winter coats. Antiquated though it was, this practice was by no means obsolete by the time Kelly Chamandy decided to enter the market in the 1940s. He promptly opened a store in the hamlet of Ramore, Ontario, located about 200 miles south of Moosonee, and began to make his own bear grease, rendering the fat of black bears he killed in the late summer or early fall, right before hibernation, in a washtub over his cabin's wood stove. No sooner had he set up shop than his bottles began to fly off the shelf. In no time, Kelly Chamandy was selling his exotic commodity to clients from all over North America, the going price being $1.50 for an eight-ounce jar.

"I don't claim that bear grease grows hair, nor cures aches and pains," Kelly Chamandy once said of his pungent product. "But my customers claim it does. Who am I to call them liars?"

One Manitoba newspaper quoted him as saying: "I got bald as a billiard ball myself in the air force during the war, when I could not get the grease. Now my own hair is starting to come back. Maybe it's the change of diet, but then again, maybe it's the bear grease."

Although Kelly may not have outright ascribed his bear grease with follicle-friendly features, he was not beyond dropping some not-so-subtle hints to the same effect. "Have you ever seen a bald-headed Indian?" he would often ask tourists, before explaining that natives from the prairies to the Great Lakes would often work bear oil into their long hair to make it shine.

Baldness was not the only ailment for which Kelly Chamandy's bear oil was used to affect a cure. Customers also used the grease to combat rheumatism, arthritis, and muscle aches, and applied it as a lubricant, waterproofing agent, and conditioner to everything from fishing lines to boot leather.

Kelly Chamandy soon expanded his product line, becoming Canada's only licensed purveyor of bear, beaver, muskrat, and raccoon meat. He sold his bear and beaver meat at 35 cents a pound, and retailed his untanned pelts for up to $25. He also sold bear gallbladders and left forepaws to Chinese merchants, bear bile and bear paw soup being rare and expensive ingredients in traditional Chinese medicine, as well as live black bear cubs, whom gas station, restaurant, and hotel owners purchased in the hope of attracting patrons to their establishments. Soon, Kelly's profits allowed him to open a gas station, a trading post, a general store, and a museum, his main articles for sale and display being Inuit soapstone and ivory carvings which he purchased from his old fur trade friends.

The Giant Owl

In the spring of 1951, Kelly Chamandy offered a $100 reward to anyone who could bring him the carcass of an enormous black bird that had been harassing Northern Ontario livestock; apparently, he thought that the monster would make a nice addition to his museum. Ted Lind and Howard McDonald were two farmers who claimed to have seen the bird about 50 miles east of Timmins, Ontario (i.e. in the vicinity of Ramore). They described the bird as having huge talons, a hooked beak, jet black feathers, and the likeness of an owl, and claimed that it was four feet tall with a 9-foot wingspan. Lind suspected that the avian colossus had snatched up fish and meat that he had strung up beyond the reach of wolves; all that survived of his catch were the tattered remains of the half-inch rope from which he had suspended it. Chamandy himself maintained that the bird had yellow eyes "the size of silver dollars", and was "large enough to carry off a small cow".

Within a few days, Kelly Chamandy upped the bounty to $150 on the condition that the bird be captured alive. According to an article in the *Pittsburgh Press*, the entrepreneur feared that his initial offer would prompt locals to "commit wholesale slaughter of birds, shooting first and examining them afterwards". To the best of this author's knowledge, the fate of the monstrous bird remains a mystery.

Marketing Schemes

The international attention garnered by his big bird bounty may have inspired a series of ingenious marketing ploys which Kelly Chamandy conducted in the 1950s, in which he sent bottles of his bear oil to famous public figures. In around 1951, for example, he sent a large bottle of bear grease to U.S. President Harry S. Truman, whose receding hairline had attracted his attention. "I got no answer from the

President," Chamandy once said of the scheme, "but the grease wasn't returned."

Later on, in 1952, Kelly sent a jar to U.S. Army General Dwight D. Eisenhower as an inauguration present (Eisenhower was elected U.S. President in the fall of 1952). He never received a reply.

Two years later, in the summer of 1954, Kelly sent a bottle of bear grease to Prince Philip, Duke of Edinburgh, whose hair appeared to be thinning. This time, he promptly received a Royal letter from the Honourable Michael Parker, the Duke's Private Secretary, thanking him for his concern and assuring him that "there is no cause for worry".

Later Life

In the 1960s, the middle-aged entrepreneur relocated with his wife to the city of Kitchener, Ontario, in order to be closer to his two children, both of whom had moved there. There, he began selling some of his old Inuit art to high-end gift shops. "The prices I can get for this stuff today..." he remarked to a journalist, shaking his head in amazement. "I remember when my store was half full of it and I couldn't *give* it away."

On February 24, 1966, after successfully bidding for a truckload of abandoned bicycles at a police auction, 64-year-old Kelly Chamandy suddenly died of a heart attack, leaving behind his wife, Frances; his children, Monty and Ulna; and a legacy of happy customers with heads full of hair and hearts full of gratitude for the services rendered by Canada's last bear oil salesman.

A Pleasant Surprise

About a month after he published this article on the website MysteriesOfCanada.com, the author of this book received an email from one Monty Chamandy. The message reads:

"Hi Hammerson,

"I am the Monty you refer to in the article- and I do not know when you wrote it. It was well researched and written and I just wanted to thank you for keeping some of our history alive. Our life was filled with adventure as you can imagine and you have a few of the many interesting parts of our exciting life. You may be interested in knowing that he, too, carved totem poles.

"Thanks again,

"Monty Chamandy"

MAD SCIENTISTS

GRANGER TAYLOR: THE SPACEMAN OF VANCOUVER ISLAND

ALTHOUGH BETTER KNOWN for its hockey players and comedians, Canada has a long and proud history of producing world-class scientists whose discoveries and inventions caused paradigm shifts in their respective fields. From Sir Frederick Banting, whose 1921 discovery of insulin revolutionized treatment for diabetes, to the engineers of SPAR Aerospace, who invented the Canadarm for use on NASA's Space Shuttle and the International Space Station, Canada's most famous scientists are generally held in high esteem throughout the scholarly world.

Like all erudite societies, Canada's scientific community has had a few of its own black sheep- eccentric pioneers who operated on the fringe of accepted practice and refused to play by the rules, whose controversial theories and bizarre experiments straddled the narrow border between genius and insanity. These tragic characters are defined by their utter consumption by a single driving obsession- a particular goal which remained just beyond their grasp, the realization of which might have conferred upon them Edison-like acclaim, their failure to accomplish which consigned them to the exotic obscurity that is the lot of the 'mad scientist'. Whether they were ahead of their time or simply stuck on a road to nowhere, these modern-day alchemists, despite embodying all the ingenuity, determination, and raw brilliance of the greatest of inventors, never had the pleasure of seeing their work come to fruition.

Although they may not have achieved their desired outcomes, the exploits of these colourful characters make for excellent stories that are legacies in their own right. Without further ado, here are the fascinating tales of three 'crazy' Canadian inventors.

The youngest mad scientist on our list is Granger Taylor, whose mysterious disappearance in 1980 remains one of the greatest mysteries of Vancouver Island.

Granger Ormond Taylor was born on October 7, 1948, in the logging and fishing town of Duncan, British Columbia, situated on the southeastern shores of Vancouver Island about halfway between Victoria and Nanaimo. His biological father died when he was an infant, having drowned in northwesterly Horne Lake during a vacation at the family cabin. When he was two years old, Granger's mother, Grace, married a widower named Jim Taylor, who had children of his own.

Granger spent his earliest years growing up with his seven siblings, which included three biological siblings, three stepsiblings, and a half-brother.

From an early age, it became clear to Mr. and Mrs. Taylor that Granger was an unusual child. He was withdrawn and socially awkward, but what he lacked in social skills he more than made up for in an extraordinary aptitude and appetite for mechanics. Granger spent much of his childhood alone in his bedroom, dismantling toy gadgets in an effort to understand their inner workings.

Despite his considerable intelligence, Granger displayed little interest in his studies and dropped out of school after completing Grade 8. He began working as an apprentice for his neighbour, an auto mechanic, and eagerly absorbed all the knowledge the old tradesman could impart. After a mere year of apprenticeship, Granger decided that he had acquired all the skills necessary for him to strike out on his own. He set up shop on his parents' forest-side property and began to tinker away on his own unconventional projects, many of which he would go on to sell to collectors or the provincial government for impressive sums of money.

It soon became evident that Granger Taylor had found his calling. At the age of fourteen, he built a single-cylinder automobile, which is now on display at Duncan's B.C. Forest Discovery Centre. Three years later, he rebuilt an abandoned bulldozer that professional heavy duty mechanics had dismissed as unsalvageable. In his early twenties, he decided to resurrect a derelict steam locomotive he found rusting in the rainforest, with alder trees growing through the chassis. It took Granger two years to restore the train to full working order, whereupon he laid tracks for it through his parents' garden and began taking neighbourhood children for rides in it, his workshop having become something of a local attraction. It seemed that there was no mechanical mystery too daunting for Granger Taylor; no kinetic conundrum he couldn't conquer.

On New Years' Eve, 1969, about half a year after Granger had finished hauling the last piece of his rusted train onto his parents' property, something strange took place at the Cowichan District Hospital not too from Granger's home. At about 5:00 in the morning, while tending to patients in the geriatric wing, four nurses working night-shift allegedly saw a silent, brilliantly-lit flying saucer hovering outside the window about three stories off the ground, near the children's ward. Doreen Kendall, the first nurse to observe the object, claimed to have witnessed two humanoid pilots standing in the craft's cockpit through its transparent window. The nurses gazed in amazement as the craft drifted behind a grove of trees before zipping away into the night sky like a shooting star.

Later that morning and throughout the following night, citizens from all over Duncan and the surrounding area, including a handful of elementary school teachers and a pilot of the Royal Canadian Naval Air Service, came forward with reports of a similar-looking UFO spotted throughout the region. For months following the incidents, flying saucers and visitors from outer space were the talk of southwestern Vancouver Island.

It seems likely that Granger Taylor was bitten by the same UFO bug that had smitten so many of his fellow Islanders in early 1970s. Not long after he applied the finishing touches to his steam locomotive, he apparently developed an interest in the dynamics of air travel, earning his pilot's license and beginning restorative work on a scrapped WWII Kittyhawk fighter plane, which he would eventually sell to a private collector for $20,000.

By the late 1970s, Granger had wearied of conventional mechanics, which no longer seemed to challenge him. Instead, he turned his attention to the greatest aeronautical question of all- the propulsion of flying saucers. No engineer on earth had yet been able to conceive an engine which could enable a huge metallic disk to maneuver as tightly, rapidly, and silently through the air as the flying saucers described by UFO witnesses. Granger Taylor decided to tackle this enigma, which had apparently baffled the most brilliant minds of military aerospace, and start on his *magnum opus*– the construction of a real-life flying saucer.

Granger Taylor began his quest by building a private office the same size and shape as the quintessential UFO. Aided by the children and teenagers who often came to watch him work, he scavenged two radio tower satellite dishes from the local dump and constructed a cylindrical building at the edge of his parents' garden, which he erected on stilts. After decorating the sides of the metallic structure with a lightning bolt design and a port-like window, he outfitted his UFO with a cast iron wood burning stove, a couch, and a television. Finally, Granger stocked his new study with science fiction novels and pseudoscientific books on UFOs, which were intended to stimulate his ingenuity. His office complete, the mechanical genius hunkered down with his books and his notes and began to consider the question of UFO propulsion.

Throughout 1979 and 1980, Granger Taylor spent much of his time alone in his backyard UFO, sitting in quiet contemplation or pouring through his many books. Then, after many months of deep pondering, something extraordinary happened. One night, while lying in bed, Granger was purportedly contacted by extraterrestrials.

According to Robert Keller- a troubled teenager whom Granger had taken under his wing, and one of the few souls with whom he shared his incredible experience- Granger explained that beings from beyond our solar system had introduced themselves to him telepathically. In the months preceding the incident, the machinist had attempted to contact extraterrestrials via a sort of radio he had devised. Perhaps, he surmised, his willingness to communicate was what prompted the aliens to choose him.

Granger would go on to have several more alleged telepathic conversations with the extraterrestrials. During these incidents, he repeatedly asked the aliens questions about the propulsion source of their saucer-like vehicles, but all they divulged was that the secret had something to do with magnetism.

In October 1980, an elated Granger Taylor confided in Keller and another friend named Bob Nielsen that the aliens had invited him on a trip through the Milky Way Galaxy. His younger friends couldn't entirely believe Granger's story, suspecting that the eccentric genius had simply experienced a strange dream or some sort of hallucination, but they couldn't entirely discount it either; if an extraterrestrial intelligence were to contact anyone on earth, they believed that Granger would undoubtedly be their first choice. Despite their earnest entreaties, Granger refused to take his eager friends with him on his upcoming interstellar voyage, claiming they had too much to leave behind on earth. He disclosed that the aliens planned to pick him up on a rainy night so that the general public wouldn't see their spaceship.

About a month later, on November 29, 1980, the town of Duncan was rocked by what newspapers dubbed 'The Storm of the Century'. Thunder, lightning, torrential rain, and gale-force winds descended upon the city, uprooting trees and downing power lines.

At 6:00 that evening, right before the height of the storm, Granger Taylor paid a visit to Bob's Grill, one of his favourite haunts. The waitress who served him his meal noticed that Granger was clad in his usual attire, consisting of jeans, logging boots, and a brown knitted sweater. He didn't have a coat with him, and was clearly ill-prepared for the incoming tempest.

At 6:30, 32-year-old Granger Taylor paid his bill, left the diner, and drove off in his 1972 light blue Datsun truck. He was never seen again.

The following day, as the people of Duncan were busy clearing their roads and driveways of fallen trees and windblown debris, Taylor's parents discovered that their son was missing. Jim Taylor found Granger's last note to the world taped to his and Grace's bedroom door. This bizarre document read:

"Dear Mother and Father,

"I have gone away to walk aboard an alien ship, as recurring dreams assured a 42-month interstellar voyage to explore the vast universe, then return.

"I am leaving behind all my possessions to you as I will no longer require the use of any. Please use the instructions in my will as a guide to help.

"Love,

"Granger"

On the back of the note was a hand-drawn map which some have interpreted as a depiction of Waterloo Mountain, located about fifteen kilometres (10 miles) southwest of the Taylor home.

Jim Taylor and his sons searched high and low for Granger, checking hospitals and driving lonely logging roads in the hope of finding some clue as to the eccentric genius' whereabouts. In accordance with his note, they looked through his will and found that he had replaced the word "deceased" with "departed" throughout the document. Try as they might, however, they could find no trace of the missing man nor his blue Datsun truck.

Months turned into years, yet the fate of Granger Taylor remained as mysterious as it had been on that fateful morning of November 30, 1980. On June 29, 1983- the date of Granger's scheduled return from his trip through the cosmos- Granger's stepbrother, Douglas Taylor, who worked for the Canadian Coast Guard at the time, sat out for half the night on the deck of his patrol boat, scanning the night sky for any sign of Granger and his alien spacecraft. His heart was heavy when he turned in for the night, the promised ship having failed to appear.

In April 1986, six years after Granger's disappearance, a municipal works crew discovered an artificial crater several meters in diameter off Mount Prevost Road, on the slopes of either Mount Prevost or northeasterly Sicker Mountain, both of which overlook northwestern Duncan. Scattered in the vicinity of the crater were rusted and discoloured fragments of what appeared to have once been a truck. The local Royal

Canadian Mounted Police subsequently investigated the scene and discovered two shards of what proved to be human bone not far from the depression. Many Duncan residents, including the police and several members of Granger's family, believed that these bones constituted the last remains of Granger Taylor. As DNA profiling was in its infancy at the time and unavailable to the Force on Vancouver Island, that suspicion was never definitively confirmed or refuted.

In the wake of the sobering discovery, a number of theories were put forth pertaining to Granger Taylor's last moments on earth. Many believed that on the night of November 29, 1980, Granger had packed his Datsun full of dynamite, which he used for removing tree stumps, driven into the wilderness, and either deliberately or accidentally blown himself and his vehicle to smithereens.

Some believed that Granger's inability to solve the mystery of flying saucer propulsion had eaten away at him during the long hours of self-imposed isolation that typified his final months. Unable to cope with his failure, he set out with the intention of taking his own life, concocting the tale of his interstellar voyage in an attempt to ease the pain of the friends and family he would leave behind.

Others have suggested that, like the ill-fated Heaven's Gate cult whose members committed mass-suicide in 1997, Taylor may have been under the misguided impression that he would need to leave his earthly body in order to board the spaceship he believed had come to take him away, and had set out to achieve that purpose.

Some of those who knew him best, however, were adamant that Granger Taylor was not suicidal. If he did blow himself up with dynamite, then it must have been accidental. Perhaps he had brought dynamite into the wilderness with the intention of using it in some way to inform the extraterrestrial astronauts of his whereabouts, or to somehow facilitate his journey into outer space. Through some terrible accident, the explosives had detonated prematurely.

Others still, however, including Granger Taylor's late mother, Grace, and his friend Robert Keller, believe that Granger Taylor was picked up by extraterrestrials on that stormy November night, just like he said he would be. Perhaps he is still hurtling through outer space in an alien spacecraft, exploring the galaxy and studying alien astronautics to his heart's content. After all, according to Albert Einstein's theory of relatively, time dilates for objects travelling near the speed of light. Perhaps one day a 35-year-old Granger Taylor will return from his 42-month voyage to find a very different Duncan to the one he left, where phones are cordless, cars drive on their own, and residents still puzzle over the fate of that quirky genius who disappeared on a stormy night so long ago.

TOM SUKANEN: THE CRAZY FINN OF SASKATCHEWAN

I F YOU DRIVE ABOUT 10 kilometres south of Moose Jaw, Saskatchewan, on the #2 Highway, you might notice a strip of antiquated buildings reminiscent of an early 1900's Saskatchewan farming village located on a dirt road to the right. This village- a collection of restored historical buildings hauled from the surrounding area- is the Sukanen Ship Pioneer Village and Museum. At the end of the village closest to the highway is a steamboat complete with a white cabin, red hull, and blue keel- a vessel christened the *Sontiainen*, more popularly known as the Sukanen Ship. This peculiar prairie ship- located more than a thousand kilometers from the nearest ocean- is the legacy of Tom Sukanen, an extraordinary Finnish-Canadian pioneer with an equally peculiar story.

The Land of Opportunity

"Tom Sukanen" was born Tomi Jannus Alankola in the small village of Kurjenkyla, Finland, on September 23, 1878. Although little is known about his early life, amateur historians know from anecdotal evidence that Tomi, in his adolescence, apprenticed as a shipwright. In these early years, Tomi learned to build wooden ships, craft steel hulls, assemble steam engines, and combine the three components to create steamships. He also learned how to calculate latitude and longitude with a sextant, a skill that he purportedly honed on numerous nautical expeditions in the frigid Baltic, Barents and Norwegian Seas.

In 1898, 20-year-old Tomi, like thousands of young Scandinavians, boarded a steamship to America, the Land of Opportunity. He dreamed of a triumphant return to his homeland, with a large family and a small fortune. To help his prospects, he anglicized his name to Tom Sukanen.

In America, Sukanen- who was, by all accounts, a giant of a man in both size and ability- searched for a steel-working job, but met with little success. His quest took him to Minnesota, where he happened upon a young second-generation Finnish woman who was struggling to manage her late father's farm. Sukanen married the girl and took up farming.

According to another version of the tale, 28-year-old Sukanen married Sanna Liisa Rintala in Finland in 1906. Soon after, he sailed for America to avoid conscription in the Imperial Russian Army (at that time, Finland was a Grand Duchy in the Russian Empire), leaving his wife, pregnant with one of his daughters, at home in Finland.

The next year, Sukanen's wife and baby daughter joined him in America. His wife, Sanna, had not responded well to his desertion, and had developed severe depression, and perhaps dementia, so debilitating that it prevented her from properly taking care of her infant daughter. To make matters worse, Sukanen refused to support his ailing wife and daughter, and accordingly spent three months in prison for his negligence. After serving his sentence, Sukanen immediately left Biwabik and embarked on his trek to Canada.

By 1911, Sukanen and his wife, relatively destitute in spite of their efforts, had a son and three daughters. That year, Sukanen, on a whim, decided to travel north to Canada in search of his brother, Svant, who had a farm in the Macrorie-Birsay area about 90-110 kilometers south of Saskatoon, Saskatchewan (roughly halfway between Saskatoon and Swift Current), where the Canadian government was still offering free land in an effort to attract settlers. He hoped to take advantage of the opportunity, file a homestead, and immigrate to Canada with his family. With his effects on his back, he left Minnesota and, using the navigational skills he had acquired as an apprentice shipwright in Finland, made the 1000-kilometre journey across the prairie to south-central Saskatchewan on foot.

Upon arriving at the Macrorie-Birsay homestead and reuniting with his brother, Svante, Sukanen decided to start his own homestead about sixteen miles away. While waiting to receive clear title to his homestead, he ingratiated himself with his fellow homesteaders by helping them with their carpentry work, farm work, and machine repairs. A mechanical genius, Sukanen also built a number of home-made machines himself, including a small wooden steam-powered threshing machine, which he lent to his neighbours, and a sewing machine, which he lent to his neighbours' wives. For himself, he constructed a tricycle, a wheat-puffing machine, and a handmade violin (Sukanen was reputed to be a proficient fiddler).

Soon, Sukanen received his homestead and began to work his own fields. His first few harvests were bountiful, and in time he acquired a respectable herd of livestock in addition to a minor fortune. During this time, the Finnish giant was sometimes seen manually hauling enormous loads of supplies from the store in Macrorie to his homestead, located ten kilometers away.

By 1918, Sukanen was making a comfortable living, and decided to return to Minnesota to collect his wife and children and bring them to Canada. Again, he made the journey on foot. Upon arriving in Minnesota, Sukanen discovered that his wife was dead. Years earlier, she had been committed to a psychiatric hospital in Fergus Falls, MN, where she expired after contracting the Spanish flu (according to another source, Sanna died in the asylum in 1914, four years before the 1918 international flu pandemic). Sukanen's children, whose mother had been unable to care for them, had long since been put up for adoption. His two oldest daughters were adopted by one family, while his son and youngest daughter were both adopted by another.

Sukanen tracked down his son and convinced him to accompany him to Canada. The pair set out on the long trek to Sukanen's homestead, but were accosted at the Canadian-American border. The American authorities promptly returned the boy to his foster family (according to another source, the boy was put in a reform school) and threatened Sukanen with jail time if he ever attempted to smuggle his son out of the country again. Crestfallen, Sukanen returned to his homestead alone.

A New Ambition

Back in 1911, when Sukanen first set sail for the New World, he pictured himself returning to Finland one day with a wife and children. With his wife dead and children relocated, that dream was no longer realistic. Aimless and confused, Sukanen decided to distract himself by joining a rail gang. While labouring for the CPR, the big Finn amazed his foremen and fellow workers by singlehandedly unloading massive steel rails from the train cart- a job typically performed by at least three men.

As his body worked, his mind drifted, and over time Sukanen formulated his next big idea. Although he couldn't return to Finland with a family anymore, he could still return in triumph. He envisioned himself a sea captain, drifting into the Port of Helsinki at the wheel of a seaworthy steamship, every inch of which he, himself, had personally handcrafted.

Before Sukanen could wholeheartedly dedicate himself to the realization of his new dream, he had to determine whether or not it was feasible. In the summer of 1929, the 51-year-old appropriated a number of river maps from the Regina Department of Archives, built a sturdy rowboat and, without saying a word to his neighbours, set off down the South Saskatchewan River. He rode the current past Saskatoon and through Prince Albert, east of which the South Saskatchewan and North Saskatchewan merged to form the Saskatchewan River. He braved the white water near Grand Rapids, Manitoba, and followed the river into Cedar Lake and across the huge Lake Winnipeg beyond. After maneuvering his craft through a series of smaller Manitoban lakes, he entered the Nelson River and rowed his way northeast to Hudson Bay. There, the seaman secured a job on a freight steamer and worked his passage to Finland, where he spent some time with his family before returning to Saskatchewan.

Immediately upon returning to his homestead, the middle-aged Finn ordered huge shipments of raw materials, including massive steel sheets, thick steel rods, stout seasoned timbers, and thousands of nails and bolts. Satisfied that his venture was feasible, Sukanen began to build his ship.

The Great Depression

When his raw materials arrived at the Macrorie rail station, Sukanen, satisfied that he could sail a ship from Saskatchewan to Finland, got to work immediately. He planned to build the steamship's deck cabins, hull, and keel separately, to float them downriver on a motorized raft, and to assemble them on the shores of Hudson Bay. First, Sukanen constructed the steam boiler. Equipped with little more than a hacksaw, a homemade forge, an anvil, and two stunted sledgehammers, the enormous Scandinavian cut half-inch-thick steel sheets to size and pounded them into cylindrical compliance. Next, he built the engine, forging all the individual components by hand. After completing the engine- a feat which, according to a CPR engineer who beheld it years later, would normally be accomplished with the use of a huge press- he set to work constructing the hull, and later the keel. Seemingly indefatigable, he laboured on his ship all day and well into the evening whenever his farming duties and Christian obligation permitted. Eventually, he neglected the farm work entirely and worked on his steamboat fulltime.

The incessant ringing of Sukanen's hammer, coupled with the surfeit of supplies that constantly appeared at the rail station, piqued the curiosity of Sukanen's neighbours. Throughout the early-mid 1930's, curious farmers flocked from the surrounding countryside to marvel at the eccentric Finn and his crazy project. Eventually, their initial good-natured bewilderment gave way to bitter resentment, blowing away with the topsoil of their fields in the devastating dust storms that characterized the "Dirty Thirties". They wondered how this brilliant man, in good conscience, could expend his considerable savings on such a ridiculous project in the midst of such widespread poverty. Whenever confronted with his apparent selfishness and the frivolity of his enterprise, Sukanen, deadpan, would wave his hand at the dusty, arid prairie and declare, with a sort of droll gravity typical of Scandinavian humour, that a great flood was coming, and that he would sail away to Finland when it came. In time, Sukanen, once a respected homesteader admired for his ingenuity and resourcefulness, degenerated into a despised recluse; the "Crazy Finn"; the Noah of the Plains.

Sukanen's health deteriorated with his reputation. Completely absorbed with his work, the Scandinavian neglected his physical appearance; his face and clothing were perpetually black from the soot of his forge. Having exhausted all of his savings on supplies, Sukanen tore apart his barn, granaries, and house for lumber, and started living in the cabins (or, according to some sources, under the hull) of his ship. Impoverished and purportedly too proud to accept charity, he subsisted on a meager diet of wheat kernels and rotten horseflesh. Malnutrition took its toll, and Sukanen lost a huge amount of weight, and much of his legendary strength along with it.

After seven years of hard labour, Sukanen had nearly completed his ship. He nailed thick tin plates (in another version, sheets of galvanized iron) to the keel to fortify it against arctic ice, and coated them in horse blood, an anticorrosion agent used by Finlanders for centuries. In a display of wry, self-deprecating wit, a characteristic for which Finns are famous, Sukanen christened his steamboat the "*Sontiainen*"- Finnish for "Little Dung Beetle."

In 1938, Sukanen asked a neighbour, who owned a tractor, to help him move the keel and hull twenty seven miles to the river, where he had already moved the deck cabins in which he was living. To spite the pariah, and perhaps to save himself social condemnation, the farmer refused. Disheartened, Sukanen attempted to move the parts himself. First, he harnessed his few starving horses to the structures. When that failed, he resorted to dragging the hull and keel himself, using a makeshift winch and a set of iron wheels.

Although Sukanen made a little progress each day, he was a mere husk of his former self, and his famous strength was quickly waning. He became increasingly depressed. Eventually, Svant, concerned for his brother's health, entreated the RCMP to bring Sukanen to an institution where he could recover his mental and physical strength and so, in

1930, RCMP Constable Bert Fisk accompanied Svante and his son Elmer to Sukanen's homestead. There, they collected Sukanen, now too weak to stand on his own, and drove him to a mental hospital in North Battleford, Saskatchewan (about 130 kilometres northwest of Saskatoon). In the end, he had moved the hull and keel less than five kilometres.

At the mental hospital, Sukanen slowly began to recover while being fed a steady diet consisting predominantly of raw fish, a Finnish staple. During this time, he wrote a strange, prophetic letter to his sister, who was living at that time in Spencer, Massachusetts. An excerpt from this letter reads:

"Four times there will be men who will try to raise and assemble this ship. Three times they will fail, but a fourth man will succeed. He will start the raising of my ship and it will sail across the prairies at speeds unheard of in this day and age, and will disappear in a mighty roar. My ship will go up and I shall rest in peace."

One day, in the spring of 1943, Sukanen learned that his ship had been disassembled and looted by vandals, and that his tools and gear had been stolen. Heartbroken and purposeless, the Finnish giant died in the asylum shortly thereafter, on April 23, 1943. His body was interred in the North Battleford cemetery.

The Prophecies

In the four decades following Sukanen's death, two of two of his prophecies would be realized.

The first, in a grotesque twist of fate, came true mere months after his death. The "great flood" that Sukanen had foretold, albeit facetiously, in the height of the Great Depression came to Saskatchewan in the summer of 1943.

The second, manifest in Sukanen's cryptic letter to his sister, came true much later. In his letter, the Finn predicted that three men would attempt to raise his ship and fail. Upon his death, one of Sukanen's few friends, a farmer named Victor Markkula, purchased what remained of the *Sontiainen* from the Macrorie municipality and stored it on his property. Victor's son, Wilf, inherited the ship sections along with the farm after promising his father to keep them safe until the right man came along to put them back together. Wilf, who went on to own a hotel in White Bear, Saskatchewan (a hamlet located about 73 kilometers northwest of Swift Current, near the Great Sand Hills), dutifully kept his father's farm and the remains of Sukanen's steamboat, which he used to house chickens and store wheat. Over the years, three different men approached him with a desire to purchase and remove the *Sontiainen*. These three, as the prophecy foretold, failed in their endeavors; two ran out of money, and the third abandoned his undertaking after the South Saskatchewan River Valley flooded.

The fourth man, Laurence T. "Moon" Mullin- an antique collector who purportedly worked as a messenger for Al Capone's henchmen in the tunnels of Moose Jaw in the 1920's- came on the scene sometime later. He had heard rumors about the fabled "Sukanen Ship" and, as an antique collector, was naturally curious as to its whereabouts. As it turned out, his son, on a hunting trip, ran into Wilf Markkula in White Bear and learned the location of the ship's resting place. Subsequently, Mullin met with Markkula, discovered the true tale of the Sukanen Ship, and became imbued with the same obsession that had consumed Sukanen in the 1930's. He told Markkula that he resolved to retire and spend the remainder of his life working to restore the ship and erect it as a monument dedicated to the memory of the extraordinary man who built it. Impressed by the antique collector's passion and sincerity, Markkula knew that the right man had come along, and decided to donate the ship to Mullin. True to his word, Mullin restored the *Sontiainen* and had it erected in the Pioneer Village and Museum south of Moose Jaw on the Saskatchewan Highway 2 north of Old Wives Lake, which became known thereafter as the Sukanen Ship Pioneer Village and Museum. True to Sukanen's prophecy, on the day the restored *Sontiainen* was loaded onto a flatbed truck and transported to its new home, the steamboat ripped down the highway at speeds largely "unheard of" in the 1930's, and disappeared in the "mighty roar" of the truck's diesel engine.

The final part of Sukanen's prophesy was realized when Mullins had Sukanen's body exhumed from the North

Battleford cemetery and interred in a small chapel in the Pioneer Village next to his ship. Finally, Tomi could rest in peace.

Comments

Following my online publication of this article, my piece received several interesting comments which shed new and interesting light on the nature of Tom Sukanen and his impossible quest. The first of these, submitted by Mr. Ray Pulkanen, reads:

"I remember as a young lad, my Dad and I went to visit Tom, driving there with a team of horses and a buggy, as my Dad farmed land just west of Tom's homestead. Tom was living beside the hull and keel which he had managed to winch a short distance from where he had constructed them. He was not a Crazy Finn as a lot depicted him. He was just obsessed by an overwhelming dream to sail back to his native Finland. His dream was so powerful that he did not realize that he would someday run out of money and eventually he would become old and weak. There just was not the equipment to be able to move this large and heavy sailboat to the river at that time. I have hunted for many years in the valley where he lived and have felt his spirit touch me powerfully, as so many others have also felt. He had that Finnish *'Sisu'*, which is unstoppable determination. I really do admire the courage and fortitude that our pioneers and ancestors had when they opened up this untamed country we now call Canada. I am so proud and blessed to have had the opportunity to understand what kind of insurmountable obstacles and sufferings they endured to create the foundations of this great country. Let us keep our country strong and free!"

Another commenter, Mrs. Carlene Graham, wrote:

"I know this story well. My father was the fourth man, Moon Mullin. I remember standing in the school ground at Brownlee, SK, watching the ship go by on the highway. That time- although I didn't realize it at the time- was the next chapter in Tom Sukanen's story. My father became obsessed with the restoration. The entire family worked alongside my father to bring life back to the ship. It was a difficult time for us. People began to think my father was "as crazy as old Tom". But he, too, had a dream. We watched that dream come true as they raised the ship and flew the Finnish flag from her bow. My dad saw to it that Tom's story made it home to Finland. It is my understanding that there is a statue of Tom in the town he came from. My daughter's ashes rest with Tom at the museum, linking our families together in eternity."

THE TRAGEDIES OF GILBERT HEDDEN AND WELSFORD PARKER

IF YOU DRIVE AN HOUR southwest of Halifax, Nova Scotia, on the Fishermen's Memorial Highway, across the Chebucto and Aspotogan Peninsulas and down the Atlantic Coast, you'll come to the picturesque little community of Western Shore. Just east of this hamlet, in the waters of Mahone Bay, lies a tiny forested isle known as Oak Island, the site of Canada's longest-running treasure hunt.

In 1795, so the legend goes, three locals named Daniel McGinnis, John Smith, and Anthony Vaughan discovered a strange depression in the soil on the island's eastern end. Beside the depression stood a massive oak tree, one of the limbs of which extended over top of the concavity. From that limb, directly in the centre of the depression, depended a rusted and rotting block and tackle.

Subsequent investigation revealed the depression to be the top of a deep backfilled shaft in which platforms of oak logs rested at regular 10-foot intervals. Knowing that Mahone

Bay, in centuries past, had served as a haven for privateers, the locals suspected that the pit might be the depository of pirate loot.

Ever since this tantalizing discovery of what has since been dubbed the 'Money Pit', treasure hunters from all over Canada and the United States have tried their hands at retrieving the shaft's mysterious contents, only to be thwarted by what appear to be brilliantly-engineered underground flood traps, catastrophic subterranean collapses, and uncannily disproportionate bad luck. To date, Oak Island's elusive treasure remains undiscovered, and its nature and the identities of whose who buried it remain a mystery.

Over the past two centuries, exasperated treasure hunters, unable to solve the riddle of the Money Pit through conventional methods, have resorted to all manner of unorthodox solutions in their efforts to locate the island's slippery spendables. Dowsing rods, automatic writing, psychics, and séances have all been employed by desperate searchers for whom the finest modern technology failed to deliver. Of all these bizarre recourses, by far the most exotic were those taken by Oak Island treasure hunter Gilbert Hedden throughout the year 1937.

Gilbert Hedden was a wealthy New Jersey-based steel manufacturer who took up the Oak Island treasure hunt in 1934. Blessed with a mechanical mind and educated in engineering, Hedden considered himself equal to the task of unlocking Oak Island's secrets. After three frustrating years of spinning his wheels, however, the hard-headed American was ready to take any help he could get, conventional or otherwise.

In 1937, Hedden descended into the realm of the obscure, taking three bizarre avenues in a last-ditch attempt to solve the Oak Island mystery. In order to fully appreciate the first of these colourful recourses, we must first come to a more thorough understanding of the lore surrounding Oak Island and one of the earliest theories regarding the nature of its treasure.

When Daniel McGinnis, John Smith, and Anthony Vaughan first discovered Oak Island's so-called 'Money Pit' in 1795, they initially suspected that they had stumbled upon a cache of long-forgotten pirate loot. From the 16th Century to the late 18th Century, Mahone Bay, in which Oak Island is located, had been a frequent haunt of pirates, and as a result, local yarns of lost pirate plunder abounded. One particular legend favoured by the early settlers of nearby Chester, Nova Scotia, was that surrounding Captain William Kidd- a 17th Century Scottish privateer who, prior to his execution for piracy in 1701, is said to have buried a fabulous treasure on some undisclosed island. Following the discovery of the Money Pit, many locals believed Oak Island to be the repository of Captain Kidd's legendary treasure.

The Tale of Captain Kidd

The tale of Captain Kidd begins in 1688- a momentous year in English history. The British throne was occupied by King James II, a Catholic monarch. At that time, most of England- and, more importantly, most members of the English Parliament- were Protestant, and many of them had little love for their Catholic king. Determined to put a fellow Protestant on the British throne, a cabal of Parliamentarians secretly plotted with King James' nephew and son-in-law, Prince William III of the Netherlands. Their scheme resulted in a successful *coup d'etat* in which Prince William, with a fleet of 600 ships and 40,000 mercenaries, sailed through the Strait of Dover and across the English Channel. The Dutch prince and his soldiers disembarked at Torbay, marched on London, and seized the throne from King James in what the Parliamentarians dubbed the "Glorious Revolution".

Although the deposed King James had been on friendly terms with Louis XIV, the powerful King of France, the Dutch prince-turned-King of England was an old and bitter enemy of the French monarch. Immediately after his coronation, King William III thrust Britain into the ongoing Nine Years' War, a conflict between France and much of continental Europe.

At that time, a mysterious 35-year-old Scottish sailor named William Kidd was at sea in the Caribbean, serving aboard a French privateering ship called the *Sainte Rose*.

Tragedies of Hedden and Parker

Since France was now at war with England, the ship's captain was given a letter of marque to capture English vessels.

Naturally, Kidd and seven other patriotic British crewmembers were loath to attack fellow Englishman. Under the leadership of Kidd and a Cornish privateer named Robert Culliford, the Britons mutinied against the *Sainte Rose's* French crew, renamed the ship the *Blessed William*, and nominated Kidd their new captain.

Captain Kidd and his crew sailed the *Blessed William* into Nevis, a small English island colony about 190 nautical miles southeast of Puerto Rico, where the governor of the colony welcomed them into his own small fleet. Although the governor could not afford to pay Kidd and his crew, he allowed them to take whatever plunder might be had from any French ships and settlements they came across. And thus William Kidd became a respectable English privateer.

After a year of defending the island of Nevis from the French navy- an occupation which offered little in the way of treasure- Kidd's old friend and fellow mutineer, Robert Culliford, decided that he'd had his fill of privateering. While Kidd was ashore the island of Antigua, Culliford and the rest of the crew, tired of the strictures of licensed privateering, left the docks and sailed into the Caribbean to pursue the pirate life. Relieved of his command, Kidd boarded a ship to New

York, where he promptly married a wealthy English widow and became one of the richest men in town.

Despite being an active and upstanding member of the little colony, Kidd quickly tired of domestic life and returned to sea. For four years, he worked as a merchant captain, shipping goods to and from New England and the Caribbean, and earning himself a good reputation in the process. His new occupation did little to satisfy his appetite for adventure, and so in December 1695, William Kidd sailed for London, England, where he hoped to apply for a captain's commission in the British Royal Navy.

By pure chance, Kidd bumped into a fellow New Yorker on the streets of London- a wealthy businessman named Robert Livingston. When Kidd told Livingston of his ambition, the businessman introduced him to his Irish friend Richard Coote, the Earl of Bellomont, who also happened to be the newly-appointed Governor of New York. The two men asked Kidd if he would consider accepting a commission to lead a pirate-hunting expedition along the so-called Pirate Round, a sailing route that led across the Atlantic, around the Cape of Good Hope, past Madagascar, to the Arabian Sea and the Red Sea beyond. There, pirates plundered Indian passenger ships filled with exotic goods and wealthy Mecca-bound pilgrims, as well as the British East India Company's merchant vessels which often accompanied them- predations which strained England's valuable relationship with India's Mughal Empire.

Tragedies of Hedden and Parker

For William Kidd, the offer seemed the opportunity of a lifetime. He accepted the invitation and secured financial backing from Livingston, Coote, and four powerful English aristocrats who insisted upon the condition that they receive three quarters of any treasure that Kidd and his crew managed to acquire. Finally, King William III himself gave Captain Kidd a letter of marque reserving 10% of the loot for the British Crown, and giving Kidd royal license to capture or sink pirate ships or French vessels he came across.

Equipped with a brand new 34-cannon oared frigate called the *Adventure Galley* and accompanied by a hand-picked crew, Captain Kidd sailed down the River Thames. On the way to the sea, his men disrespected the crew of a yacht of the Royal Navy. As punishment for the offence, the yacht's captain pressed most of Kidd's sailors into naval service, leaving the Scottish captain with a barely functional skeleton crew.

Short-handed, Kidd sailed across the Atlantic to the port of New York, where he supplemented his meagre crew with a large number of hardened pirates. In order to convince these rough sailors to sign aboard his ship, Kidd agreed to give them 75% of whatever plunder they might acquire as opposed to the 25% stipulated by his license. In doing so, Kidd violated his letter of marque- a misdemeanor which would contribute to his eventual undoing.

His ranks filled, Captain Kidd set out on the Pirate Round, determined to abide by the conditions of his license. Rather than French or pirate vessels, however, Kidd and his crew met only with misfortune. On December 11th, the *Adventure Galley* was approached by a convoy of British Royal Navy men-of-war. The flotilla's commander, Commodore Thomas Warren, ordered Kidd to accompany him to the Cape of Good Hope on the southern tip of Africa, hoping to impress some of his sailors into service in his own fleet.

Rather than deliver members of his own hard-won crew to Commodore Warren, Captain Kidd decided to slip away in the night and continue on alone. This evasion led Warren to believe that Kidd and his crew had something to hide, prompting him to spread the rumour throughout the British East India Company that privateer Captain Kidd had gone rogue.

The crew of the *Adventure Galley* rounded the southern tip of Africa and sailed along the coast of Madagascar. When they failed to encounter any enemy ships in that notorious pirate haven, they sailed northwest to the Comoro Islands to patch up their ship. There, two thirds of the crew came down with dysentery. Forty of them died within a week.

When the disease ran its course and the survivors had regained sufficient strength to continue their voyage, the crew of the *Adventure Galley* headed north to hunt for pirates and Frenchmen. In late June, they arrived at the mouth of the Red Sea and lay at anchor, ready to pounce on any enemy ships that approached. By this time, Captain Kidd's crew was growing restless, and whispers of mutiny rippled throughout the decks.

Although the crew of the *Adventure Galley* never encountered any pirates in the Arabian Sea, they were fired on by English, Dutch, Portuguese, and Arabian ships whose captains thought they were pirates themselves.

Weeks turned into months, and by the fall of 1697, Kidd's crew was on the brink of mutiny. On October 30th, 1697, one of the crewmembers- a gunner named William Moore- sat on deck sharpening a chisel and muttering under his breath. When Kidd inquired as to Moore's rumblings, the gunner urged Kidd to attack a nearby Dutch ship and plunder its cargo- a flagrant act of piracy. When Kidd refused, a quarrel ensued which ended with Kidd cracking Moore over the head with an iron-ringed bucket. The blow fractured Moore's skull, and the gunner succumbed to his injury the following day.

Not long after Moore's death, Kidd and his crew, through the practice of flying false colours, managed to capture a French ship without a shot being fired- a capture in accordance with Kidd's commission. The crew of the Adventure Galley appropriated two chests of opium, twelve bales of cotton, and other odds and ends from the French vessel before continuing down the Malabar Coast of southwestern India.

On January 30th, 1698, the Scottish captain, using similar tactics, captured the massive *Quedagh Merchant*, an Indian merchant vessel loaded with silk, satin, gold, silver, jewels, and a variety of valuable East Indian goods. Kidd learned that the ship was chartered by the French East India Company and owned by a company of Armenian merchants, and was initially satisfied that this capture was a legitimate one. However, upon further investigation, he learned that the ship's captain was English, and that the vessel was part of the same Muslim fleet whose piratical predators he was tasked with combatting. Worse, a large proportion of the ship's cargo was owned by a senior official of the Mughal Empire. Kidd tried to convince his crew to return the ship's cargo, but the disgruntled sailors would have none of it. Unwilling to risk a mutiny, Kidd reluctantly acceded to their demands and set sail for New York. His capture of the *Quedagh Merchant* branded him a pirate, and his notorious reputation quickly preceded him throughout the Atlantic.

With the two freshly-captured merchant ships trailing behind them, Captain Kidd and his crew sailed across the Indian Ocean to Madagascar. Before heading home, the Scottish captain decided to pay a visit to Ile Sainte-Marie, an infamous pirate haunt off Madagascar's eastern coast. Sure enough, he found a pirate ship bobbing in the harbor- the first of its kind that he and his crew had encountered throughout their entire grueling voyage. Kidd soon learned that the frigate was captained by none other than Robert Culliford, the pirate who had mutinied against him in the Caribbean.

Hungry for revenge, the privateer donned his cutlass, loaded a brace of flintlock pistols, and asked his crew to help him take the ship. Many of his sailors were former pirates themselves however, and had come to despise their strict Scottish captain. Rather than attack Culliford, the vast majority opted to throw in their lot with the Cornish buccaneer. They defected to the other ship, leaving Kidd with a mere fifteen loyal sailors. Having miraculously retained most of their precious cargo, Captain Kidd and his tiny crew abandoned the rotting *Adventure Galley* for the *Quedagh Merchant* and headed for home.

The privateers followed trade winds across the Atlantic to the Caribbean. There, they learned that the governor of every English colony in the Americas had orders to arrest them for piracy. After bartering silks and other fabrics for provisions and a new ship, Captain Kidd followed the Gulf Stream north to New England.

Just outside the New York harbor, Kidd received word that one of his main backers, Richard Coote, the Governor of New York, had agreed to offer Kidd clemency for his piracy. In a letter, the Irish aristocrat invited Kidd to sail into Boston Harbour, where he was currently doing business. Captain Kidd decided to accept the invitation. Before heading to

Boston, however, he cached a large part of his treasure on Gardiner's Island, off the eastern shores of Long Island, New York, just in case he found himself in need of leverage.

Captain Kidd's suspicions were well founded. Less than a week after arriving in Boston Harbour, he and his crew were arrested by the local police and imprisoned in the city jail; Richard Coote, one of his major backers, had betrayed him.

Over the following year, Kidd enduring a long imprisonment followed by a hugely unfair trial in which he was convicted of piracy and the murder of his gunner, William Moore. After the verdict was passed, Kidd sent a letter to the Speaker of the English House of Commons claiming that he had hidden a hoard of treasure valued at 100,000 pounds sterling- worth twenty million American dollars today- and that he would help find it for the Crown if he was spared the noose.

His entreaty fell on deaf ears. On May 23rd, 1701, at London's Execution Dock, Captain William Kidd was hanged. His body was then suspended in a gibbet over the River Thames for three years as a warning to pirates.

Captain Kidd's Treasure

Following Kidd's execution, Englishmen throughout the British Empire speculated as to the nature and whereabouts of the treasure the pirate captain claimed to have hidden. Could Kidd have invented the tale as a desperate attempt to delay his appointment with the hangman? Or was there truly a hoard of gold and silver hidden away on some lonely shore, just waiting to be discovered?

Legend has it that, half a century later, in the mid-1700s, an old sailor from New England lay dying. On his deathbed, he confessed to his family that he had been a member of Captain Kidd's crew. Before passing away, he disclosed that he had helped the pirate captain bury his sizeable treasure on an island east of Boston.

Naturally, when Daniel McGinnis, John Smith, and Anthony Vaughan discovered a depression in the soil on Oak Island, with a block and tackle suspended from the oak tree that grew at its edge, they hoped that they had stumbled upon Kidd's legendary loot. So did most of the other treasure hunters to try their luck on Oak Island throughout the 19th Century.

Wilkins' Map

In 1934, the Oak Island treasure hunt was taken up by Gilbert Hedden, a retired steel manufacturer from New Jersey. His brief and exciting tenure on the island was marked by one of the most bizarre chapters in the history of Oak Island.

In 1937, Hedden's lawyer, Reginald V. Harris, read a recently-published book written by British journalist Harold T. Wilkins entitled *Captain Kidd and his Skeleton Island*. The first twelve chapters of this book describe the life of Captain Kidd and the aftermath of his execution. The next seven chapters detail various hunts for his supposed treasure. The final chapters of Wilkins' book reveal a new break in the case: the discovery of four 17th Century treasure maps said to have once belonged to Captain Kidd.

These treasure maps, Wilkins claimed, were recently discovered by a wealthy Englishman named Hubert Palmer, who collected genuine pirate artifacts as a hobby. Throughout the 1930s, Palmer acquired four pieces of 17th Century furniture bearing engravings which indicated that they once belonged to William Kidd. Within each of these artifacts was a secret compartment, and within each compartment was a treasure map depicting a particular island in the South China Sea.

At the end of his book, Wilkins included a number of photographs featuring the four pieces of antique furniture, Kidd's letter of marque, and various portraits of the notorious 17th Century pirate. Hidden among these photographs is an image of a hand-drawn treasure map with a reversed compass, which an accompanying description describes as the first chart that Palmer discovered in Captain Kidd's supposed sea chest. The map included a cryptic legend which reads:

Tragedies of Hedden and Parker

18 West and by 7 East on Rock

39 Southwest 14 North Tree

7 by 8 by 4

Reginald Harris couldn't help but notice that this treasure map, when flipped right-side up, bore remarkable resemblance to Oak Island. Even more intriguing was the fact that many of the map's features corresponded with landmarks on Oak Island. The lagoon, for example, was eerily congruent with a triangular swamp which bisects Oak Island; the elevations shown on the map were in the same locations as hills on Oak Island; and cross on the map matched the location of the Money Pit. In total, Harris identified fourteen resemblances between Wilkins' map and Oak Island, and only one minor discrepancy.

Harris showed the map to Gilbert Hedden, who was similarly fascinated by its uncanny resemblance to Oak Island. Hedden became convinced that Wilkins' chart might, in fact, be a real Oak Island treasure map drawn up by the original Money Pit builders, and so he sent a letter to Harold Wilkins voicing his suspicion.

Wilkins sent a letter back to Hedden assuring him that the treasure map in his book was not a map of Oak Island, but rather a depiction of an island in some 'eastern sea' far from the Atlantic. Hedden was unconvinced. To him, the similarities between Wilkins' map and Oak Island were

WILKINS' MAP

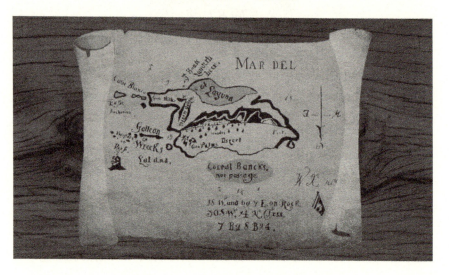

MAP OF OAK ISLAND

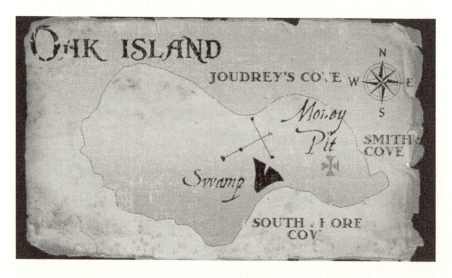

too strong to be coincidental. He then turned his attention towards the mysterious directions at the bottom of the chart.

The first line of directions seemed to suggest that the first step in the treasure hunt was to locate some sort of prominent rock, probably situated on the beach somewhere near the spot at which treasure hunters would be most likely to disembark. In the case of Oak Island, that beach was probably Smith's Cove, the section of the island most exposed to the ocean. While discussing this possibility with an elder treasure hunter named Frederick Blair, Hedden learned that two mysterious drilled rocks had been discovered on Oak Island long ago, and that one of these rocks lay on the shores of Smith's Cove. Hedden had his crew search for these stones, and sure enough, a rock with a 2-inch-deep, 1-inch-in-diameter hole was discovered at Smith's Cove. Another rock with a similar hole was subsequently found about fifty feet north of the Money Pit.

The rocks were found to be exactly 25 rods apart from one another, rods being an old English unit of measurement amounting to about five metres, or five and a half yards. Exactly seven rods west of the stone at Smith's Cove, and eighteen rods east of the western stone, lay the Cave-in Pit, a mysterious depression believed by many to be the site of an airshaft dug by the builders of one of Oak Island supposed underground flood tunnels. The Cave-in Pit appeared to be the place indicated by the first line of directions on Wilkins' map.

After making that tantalizing discovery, Hedden focused on the second line of directions. First, he had one of his employees, named Amos Nauss, run a line thirty rods southwest of the Cave-in Pit. In Nauss' words:

"Hedden gave me some idea that there was something down there at the beach that he wanted to find. So I explored around there with a hoe. I was clawing around and suddenly I hit one rock, then another and another, all in line with each other. So I decided there was something there, and I started clearing it and called Hedden over."

Nauss had rediscovered what has since been dubbed the 'stone triangle', a mysterious arrangement of beach stones on the South Shore Cove forming an arrow which pointed due north, in the direction of the Money Pit.

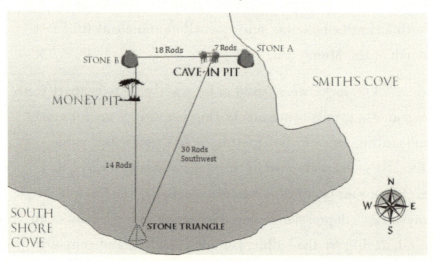

Astonished, Hedden ran a line fourteen rods north of the stone triangle. Sure enough, the line ran to the edge of the

Tragedies of Hedden and Parker

Money Pit, where legend says a large oak tree once stood. The directions on Wilkins' map seemed to apply perfectly to Oak Island.

Although he could make neither heads nor tails of the last line of directions, Hedden was convinced more than ever that the chart in Wilkins' book was a genuine Oak Island treasure map. Determined to follow this new and exciting lead, he decided to travel to England and meet Harold Wilkins in person. When Hedden informed the writer of his intentions, Wilkins wrote back that he was willing to meet with the treasure hunter, but that such a journey would be a waste of time, as the map in his book was definitely not an Oak Island treasure map. Nevertheless, Hedden made the trip to England and met with Wilkins in December, 1937, in his London hotel room outside Green Park, Piccadilly. His experience was both strange and discouraging.

Upon meeting Hedden, the English author confessed that the map in his book was, in fact, a diagram of his own devising. His publisher had demanded that he include some sort of authentic-looking treasure map in his book. Hubert Palmer, the owner of the four Captain Kidd maps which Wilkins described in his book, would not allow him to publish photos of his charts, and so Wilkins had no choice but to draw his own treasure map based on his recollection of Palmer's maps. When his publishers further stipulated that his map contain instructions on how to locate the treasure for added spice, Wilkins fabricated the three lines of directions using nothing more than his imagination.

Baffled by the remarkable connection between Wilkins' ad-libbed treasure hunting instructions and the landmarks on Oak Island, Hedden told the journalist all about the mysterious drilled stones, the stone triangle, the Cave-in Pit, and the oak tree believed to have once stood beside the Money Pit, and the uncanny relationship between these landmarks and the instructions on Wilkins' map. As Hedden explained the extraordinary coincidence, Wilkins became convinced that he must be the reincarnation of a 17th Century pirate, perhaps even Captain Kidd himself, and that his subconscious mind had conjured up some long-forgotten memory of the map leading to Kidd's lost treasure, buried on Oak Island. After Wilkins enthusiastically revealed his conviction to Hedden, the latter began to suspect that the journalist was, in his words, "every bit as crazy as his book would make him seem."

Bill Burrud's Treasure Map

Although many Oak Island enthusiasts today are familiar with the mystifying saga of the Wilkins Map, very few are acquainted with its strange follow-up - a puzzling sequel which the author of this book published for the first time in the summer of 2019, in a YouTube video entitled

Tragedies of Hedden and Parker

'*Another Wrinkle in the Wilkins Map*'. The following subchapter constitutes the script of that video's final act.

In 1958, a former child actor and WWII veteran named Bill Burrud produced a TV series entitled *Treasure*. This series was essentially a collection of documentaries on buried loot, forgotten gold mines, and lost cities. One of the episodes, incidentally, is on the mystery of Oak Island.

Another episode of *Treasure*, entitled "Shipwreck of the Dry Tortugas", follows the hunt for a shipwreck located off a deserted island located about 90 miles west of Key West, Florida, just beyond a cluster of islands called the Dry Tortugas. The episode opens with a shot of a large treasure map. The viewer may recognize this document as an augmented, coloured replica of the chart from Harold Wilkin's book *Captain Kidd and his Skeleton Island*.

In the first few minutes of the program, we are informed that the map was brought to the show's producer by one of their viewers, a Mr. David Buckner of Key West, Florida, and that it had been in Buckner's family for generations. The map allegedly shows the location of a French merchant ship which had wrecked off the island in 1883, stranding its valuable cargo on a coral reef.

After introducing us to the map, the show follows the journey of actors Gene McCabe and Lee Hanson, who set out in search of the shipwreck. First, the pair travel to Key West, where they meet with a tanned, rugged-looking skin diver named Ed Sosinksi. The treasure hunters show Sosinski their treasure map and tell him the story of the French shipwreck. The skin diver claims to know the island, locating it on his own nautical charts, and agrees to take the treasure hunters to it. With that, the three men climb aboard Sosinksi's boat and head west.

On their way to the shipwreck, the treasure hunters pay a visit to Fort Jefferson, a huge American fortress built in 1825 for the purpose of suppressing piracy in the Caribbean. There, Sosinski tells the treasure hunters that, according to legend, the sole survivor of the French shipwreck had washed ashore at Fort Jefferson clinging to a piece of wreckage. The survivor informed the fort's garrison that he and his crew were beset by a ferocious gale. Worse, they had been led aground a coral reef by mysterious signal lights which suddenly appeared at the height of the storm. No one knew where the lights came from.

On the advice of Fort Jefferson's caretaker, the treasure hunters then proceed to Bleaker's Island, named for a hermit named Vincent Bleaker who lived there in the late 1800s. According to the caretaker, rumour had it that Bleaker would stand in his beach shack during storms and hoist a lantern in the hope that some unfortunate ship would run into the coral reef that fronted his island, leaving its cargo for the taking. Perhaps, the narrator suggests, Bleaker had a hand in the demise of the French ship.

Tragedies of Hedden and Parker

After exploring the deserted island, the trio head towards their final destination. True to his word, Sosinski leads the treasure hunters to a sunken ship entombed in coral. Donning scuba gear, the treasure hunters explore the ship and recover a few interesting artifacts, including a cannonball, an old hatch cover, a swivel gun, a piece of ivory, and some sterling silver tableware. Pleased with their discoveries, the treasure hunters head for Key West as the sun begins to set.

The shipwreck that Gene McCabe, Lee Hanson, and Ed Sosinski explored in this episode of Bill Burrud's *Treasure* is undoubtedly real. The legitimacy of the treasure map which ostensibly prompted their treasure hunt, however, is another question entirely. Upon close inspection, the map appears to be artificially weathered, apparently for the purpose of making it appear older. The map, it seems, is probably a hoax intended for dramatic effect.

Somewhat more puzzling is the fact that the map appears to conform in shape with some unnamed island allegedly located off the Dry Tortugas, as evidenced by the nautical chart produced by Sosinski prior to the treasure hunt. Although the resemblance is probably coincidental, it adds yet another twist to the convoluted tale of the Wilkins Map and the most bizarre chapter in the history of the Oak Island treasure hunt.

Welsford Parker and the Mineral Wave Ray

Harold Wilkins' treasure map constitutes but one of three curious means by which Gilbert Hedden attempted to solve the riddle of Oak Island in 1937. That same year, the New Jerseyite consulted a psychic from Saginaw, Michigan, named John Wicks, who had, years earlier, informed a previous Oak Island Treasure hunter named Frederick Blair that the Money Pit was the repository of the lost treasure of Tumbez, Peru, spirited away by Incan priests during the 16th Century *Conquista* of Francisco Pizarro. Instead of shedding light on the location of Oak Island's treasure, as Hedden hoped he would, Wicks simply told the treasure hunter that "the time [was] not yet ripe" for the lost gold of the Incas to be found.

Hedden's third 1937 recourse was the 'Mineral Wave Ray', a piece of 'black box' technology with mysterious inner workings invented by Welsford R. Parker, an equally-mysterious engineer from Windsor, Nova Scotia. Parker claimed that his camera-equipped machine took photographs of objects on which it was able to pinpoint the location of hidden gold and other precious minerals. Although Hedden was dubious of the machine's ability, his lawyer, Reginald Harris, convinced him to give it a chance, claiming that a fellow lawyer vouched for its efficacy after witnessing a demonstration of the machine in his law office. Hedden allowed Parker to use the machine on Oak Island, and, after an unsuccessful test, wrote it off as "a complete and not very clever hoax".

Gilbert Hedden abandoned the Oak Island treasure hunt in 1938, passing the torch to a New York engineering professor named Erwin Hamilton. Hamilton, in turn, was succeeded by a Nova Scotian businessman named Mel Chappell, who had worked with his father on the island in the late 1800s.

In December 1950, twelve years after the 'Mineral Wave Ray's' first appearance on Oak Island, Welsford Parker, who had since relocated to Belleville, Ontario, convinced Mel Chappell to allow him to test a new and improved iteration of his machine on the island. This device consisted of a black box filled with wires, vacuum tubes, condensers, resistors, and batteries, with a camera lens attached to one end. It contained two receptacles, one of which was to hold a sample of the substance sought (ex. gold, silver, etc.), and the other being a narrow slit into which a photograph of the target area was to be slipped. The device was surmounted by a pair of rods which the operator was to hold. When the device approached any sizeable accumulation of the desired mineral, the rods were supposed to be drawn in its direction.

At Chappell's invitation, Parker wandered about the island with his machine, locating five different spots at which his device indicated the presence of buried treasure. It cost Chappell $35,000 to excavate these points of interest, none of which contained the promised loot. "I fell for it," Chappell conceded in a later reminiscence. "It looked possible to me at the time, but it turned out there was nothing to it."

Four years after Parker's second Oak Island failure, the inventor's mysterious machine came to the attention of John W. Campbell, the editor of the science fiction magazine *Astounding*. Campbell was an early (and perhaps the only true) champion of 'psionics'- a pseudo-scientific field of study revolving around the development of electronic machinery through which the practical application of psychic powers can be effected.

In the spring of 1954, Campbell met with Welsford Parker at the inventor's home in Belleville. After examining Parker's Mineral Wave Ray and listening to Parker's explanation of its mechanism, the editor became convinced of its merit. "Parker is not a fool," he wrote. "He's a brilliant pragmatic experimenter. He has stumbled onto a new, basic principle of the universe." This principal, Campbell theorized, was an "urge field" to which all human beings were intrinsically connected. The Mineral Wave Ray, he believed, allowed its operator to unconsciously, psychically locate the object of his or her desire.

Campbell suspected that Parker's machine could be used as a substitute for radio once identical devices were manufactured. Convinced of its commercial potential, he purchased ten thousand shares of stock in the inventor's company, Parker Universal Contract Ltd. Following his investment, he optimistically wrote his sister, "[A] larger-size crackpot has to be a millionaire to be a genius, and I'll be a millionaire."

Unfortunately for Campbell, Welsford Parker proved an uncooperative business partner. During his second trip to Belleville, Campbell pushed the inventor to define the terms of their arrangement, to which Parker responded by terminating their partnership. As one writer put it, "It evidently never occurred to Campbell... that a man who could spend decades working on such a device might not be the sort to work well with others..." Regrettably, Campbell remained a "crackpot" by his own definition, failing to attain the financial success which he hoped would bolster his legitimacy as a proponent of psionics. Similarly, Welsford Parker's mysterious machine failed to live up to its own hype, condemning its inventor to the shadowy status of the mad scientist.

GHOSTS OF THE GRAND RAILWAY HOTELS

GHOSTLY TALES OF THE BANFF SPRINGS HOTEL

PERHAPS THE MOST famous of all the luxury Canadian railway hotels is the Fairmont Banff Springs Hotel, located in the town of Banff, Alberta. Initially marketed towards European sportsmen and tourists seeking a luxury wilderness experience, the aptly-dubbed "Castle of the Rockies" was built at the behest of CPR president William Van Horne in 1888. Since its grand opening to the public, countless guests from all over the world- among them Marilyn Monroe, Queen Elizabeth II and Helen Keller- have checked in to the hotel. According to a number of legends ostensibly born from the first-hand accounts of hotel patrons and staff, some these guests never checked out.

The Banff Springs Hotel is home to a number of ghost stories, all of which the hotel officially denies. At least one of the Banff Springs' supposed ghostly guests is said to haunt the missing room 873 on the eighth floor. According to hotel lore, a man, while staying with his wife and young daughter in room 873, murdered his family before committing suicide. As the story goes, the spirit of the young girl- and, in some versions, the spirit of her mother- never left the room. Guests who stayed in the room after the subsequent investigation and cleanup reported being awoken in the night by violent shrieks, and chambermaids who routinely cleaned the room would report finding bloody fingerprints on the bathroom mirror that could not be washed off. In response to the disturbing reports, hotel management sealed off the room. In spite of this, some say, the ghost (or ghosts) of room 873 still haunts the vicinity of the room to this day.

Another of the permanent residents purported to walk the halls of the Banff Springs is the ghost of Sam McCauley (or McAuley), a beloved Scottish bellman who, before his death in the mid-late 1970's, swore to posthumously return to haunt his workplace. Incidents involving mysterious phantom lights, elevator doors opening and closing at random and hotel guests being helped by an elderly Scottish bellman in an antiquated uniform have been attributed to Sam's ghost.

Some other alleged hotel spectres include a ghostly bartender who encourages inebriated patrons to go to bed, and a headless man who, despite his obvious handicap, somehow manages to play the bagpipes.

Of all the ghost stories associated with the Banff Springs Hotel, perhaps the most iconic and well-known is the tale of the phantom bride. According to the legend, a young couple was married in Banff sometime in the early 1930's. It was arranged for their wedding banquet to be held in the Banff Springs Hotel, where the couple was renting the bridal suite. Before the beginning of the banquet, the newlywed bride ascended a marble staircase up to the Cascade Ballroom to join her husband, who was waiting at the top. As she did so, her wedding gown brushed against one of the candles that lined the curved staircase and caught fire. In the panic that ensued, the bride tripped over her wedding dress, fell down the flight of marble stairs, broke her neck and died.

It is said that her ghost has haunted the hotel ever since. Over the years, various hotel patrons and staff have reported seeing a phantasmal bride dancing alone in the Cascade Ballroom, or ascending the marble staircase on which the tragic incident is rumored to have taken place. Others have heard strange noises emanating from the bridal suite when the room was not in use. True or not, the tale of the ghostly bride of the Banff Springs Hotel is surrounded in an aura of mystery and romance and has become entrenched in the folklore of Canada's Rocky Mountains.

Personal Anecdotes

Following my online publication of this article, several former guests of the Banff Springs Hotel left comments on my website in which they described their own spooky experiences in the so-called 'Castle of the Rockies'.

One of the commenters was a former hotel employee named Patrick, who described another haunted staircase in the Banff Springs Hotel, the upper exit of which had been bricked off for years. During his employment, which lasted from 1981 to 1983, guests "reported hearing laughing, crying, [and] screaming from this area... As employees, we were told not to tell guests anything about this 'ghost' situation."

Another commenter, who addressed him/herself as L.B., claimed to have seen the spectral apparition of a woman and a girl in one of the hotel's hallways, and to have heard male laughter in that same hall in the middle of the night when no one was around.

Another commenter, who called herself 'Julie of Cardiff', claimed that she knew nothing of the hotel's alleged ghosts when she stayed there in 2006. One afternoon, while snoozing in her hotel bed, the room's temperature suddenly dropped. Immediately afterwards, Julie felt something grab her foot. "Never experienced anything like that before or since," she concluded.

Commenter Dell Marie Lamb claimed that she and her family once stayed at a room in the Banff Springs Hotel which was furnished with a fireplace. During a second visit to the Banff Springs, she requested a room with a fireplace, and was told by the concierge that no such rooms existed in the hotel. "I have our pictures, which were taken in front of the fireplace," she wrote, "but was told there were no rooms with fireplaces. A ghost room..."

Another commenter, who addressed herself as 'Bella', wrote: "I was just at Fairmont a couple days ago. We went for supper at Castello Italiana [a restaurant in the hotel]. After, my family and I were taking pictures in the hall outside of the restaurant. During this, I had felt something tugging on my dress, but no one was behind me and it was not possible for it to have snagged on anything. I don't know if it could have been a ghost, but I thought it was pretty cool!"

GHOSTLY TALES OF THE PRINCE OF WALES HOTEL

———◆———

IF YOU TAKE THE ALBERTA Highway 6 south from the town of Pincher Creek, you'll find yourself leaving the prairie-like Porcupine Hills for the forests and mountains of Waterton Lakes National Park. This jewel in the Rocky Mountains, tucked away in the southwest corner of Alberta across the border from its American sister, Glacier National Park, is currently recovering from the devastating effects of the Kenow Wildfire, which consumed over 19,000 hectares of Waterton wilderness in the summer of 2017. This hiccup notwithstanding, Waterton Lakes is a popular tourist destination which has hosted thousands of sportsmen and outdoor adventurers since the days of its first ranger, Kootenai Brown.

On a high windswept hill overlooking the Park's eponymous lakes stands the magnificent Prince of Wales Hotel, the last of the grand railway hotels to be built on Canadian soil. In the summer months, this historic Swiss chalet-style landmark houses guests from all over the world, come to hike the perilous Crypt Lake Trail, cruise the Lakes by boat, or simply enjoy the breathtaking scenery of the Rockies' smallest park.

In the fall and winter, the Prince of Wales lies desolate and abandoned, its windows dark, its doors boarded up, and the wind howling through gaps in its wooden exterior. In this eerie condition, the hotel appears more congruous with its many ghost stories- an attribute which all of Canada's grand railway hotels seem to share.

History

The Prince of Wales hotel was built in 1926/27 at the behest of Louis W. Hill, president of an American railroad called the Great Northern Railway. At that time, alcohol was outlawed in the United States, and many thirsty Americans made pilgrimages to the Great White North to indulge in their favourite beverages (Alberta ended its own Prohibition in 1923). Hill, who had built several grand railway hotels in neighbouring Glacier National Park, Montana, hoped that a similar hotel in Waterton might entice American liquor tourists to visit Southwestern Alberta, utilizing his railway and U.S. hotels on the journey north. It is somewhat ironic that Hill's Waterton hotel, built for the express purpose of attracting liquor tourism, is located right beside the predominantly-Mormon counties of Cardston and Warner- the only districts in Alberta where alcohol is still outlawed.

The Ghosts

Named after the (future, short-reigning) King Edward VIII in a vain attempt to entice him to stay there during his 1927 royal tour of Canada, the Prince of Wales Hotel is said to house a number of permanent residents. One of these is the ghost of the unfaithful wife of a former hotel chef who lived with her husband on the premises. According to local legend, the chef and his wife disappeared from the hotel one night without notice. The chef reappeared sometime later in British Columbia, alone. Some say that the chef murdered his wife in Room 608 of the Prince of Wales Hotel on the night of his departure. Although he managed to dispose of his wife's body, the spirit of the murdered woman remained in the room; every once in a while, patrons staying in Room 608 report being tucked into bed by unseen hands.

Although there is no historical basis for the tale of the ghost of the chef's wife, another hotel ghost story may have some merit to it. The most frequently reported unexplained phenomenon to take place at the Prince of Wales Hotel is the inexplicable aroma of tobacco smoke which occasionally wafts through the Royal Stewart Dining Room. This phantom smell is said to be associated with the ghost of a well-dressed top hat-wearing gentleman who haunts the dining room and the basement, appearing to unsuspecting guests and staff as a reflection in windows and mirrors. Although some writers have attempted to connect this spectre with a construction worker who allegedly fell from some scaffolding to his death during the hotel's construction, the image of a well-dressed tobacco smoker corresponds quite well with that of Captain Rodden S. Harrison, the hotel's first manager- a pipe smoker who frequently affected a tweed suit. Captain Harrison is said to have taken great pride in his work, and had his staff furnish the tables in the Royal Stewart Dining Room with freshly picked wildflowers every morning. Perhaps the Captain's spirit resides in the hotel to this day, enjoying the occasional after-dinner smoke and checking in on his guests from time to time.

Another of the Prince of Wales' spirits is said to haunt the lobby, where hotel staff sometimes report hearing the heavy disembodied footsteps of a man in the middle of the night. One former staff member, in an internet chatroom, confessed that he broke into the hotel in the offseason in order to spend the night there. His intrusion apparently offended this invisible resident, who raced down the stairs from the fifth or sixth floor and across the lobby towards him, effectively chasing him from the premises.

The most famous phantom of the Prince of Wales Hotel is the "Lady in White", a spectre of a young woman in a white gown said to haunt the Rooms 510 and 516. This feminine phantasm makes her presence known by locking windows left open overnight, running the taps, tapping on doors, turning the lights on, and blowing her icy breath down the necks of hapless guests. Some hotel patrons have reported hearing disembodied footsteps in the hallways or on the balconies. Others claim to have been locked out of their own rooms, finding that someone, or something, had locked the door from the inside in their absence. One guest staying in Room 516 even maintained that the apparition of a young woman slipped into bed with him and his wife in the dead of the night... before vanishing beneath the sheets.

Popular legend attributes this phantom to the spirit of a young chambermaid named Sarah, who started working at the hotel shortly after its grand opening in 1927. Sarah was in love with a member of the hotel staff. When the man rejected her advances, Sarah lapsed into despair and threw herself from a window on the fourth floor (in some versions, she jumped from the fifth or six floor). Her ghost remains in the hotel to this very day, haunting the site of her suicide.

It is likely that the legend of Sarah's ghost is based on a tragic event that took place in 1977- a particularly dark year for the Prince of Wales Hotel. In April that year, a beloved hotel handyman named Johnny Haslam died in a car accident. Later that fall, the hotel was invaded by a hoard of government inspectors sent to investigate claims of poor working conditions and allegations that the antiquated building was not up to code.

Perhaps the most tragic event to take place that year was the suicide of a 20-year-old seasonal employee from Dorval, Quebec, who worked in the hotel's giftshop. This employee, named Lorraine, had fallen in love with Clifford Hummel, the handsome and athletic manager of the Prince of Wales Hotel. When Hummel, who was already in a relationship at that time, failed to reciprocate her affections,

Lorraine was heartbroken. On Sunday, September 29th, 1977, the grief-stricken woman stripped naked and ran throughout the hotel before leaping to her death from the balcony on the hotel's sixth floor. Her broken body was discovered on the flagstone patio that overlooks the Waterton Lakes.

"[The suicide] did affect a lot of people," said Lorraine's co-worker, 18-year-old Marilyn Illerdrun, to a reporter for the *Lethbridge Herald*. "It left a bad feeling to the hotel, to the whole staff... I think it started a whole new feeling."

Although the tale of Sarah's ghost is almost certainly based on Lorraine's suicide, a woman named Sarah *was* involved in a tragic accident that took place near the Prince of Wales early in the hotel's history. On Friday, August 10, 1928, two cars collided at the foot of the hill on which the Prince of Wales stands. One of the vehicles was occupied by four passengers, one of whom was named Sarah Ann Bennett. Although Sarah walked away from the wreck with little more than a broken collar bone, the sole occupant of the other vehicle was not so fortunate; Mrs. Hiram Maughm was taken to the hospital in Cardston, Alberta, where her arm was amputated.

Whatever their origins, the ghost stories of the Prince of Wales Hotel imbue Waterton Lakes with a fitting aura of mystery and intrigue- an essential concomitant to all great Canadian national parks.

THE UNKNOWN

CANADA'S LOST WORLDS

ALL AROUND THE WORLD, folklore is replete with tales of lost lands which modern explorers have failed to relocate. Since Classical Antiquity, Greek scholars have written about Atlantis, a bygone possibly-allegorical island continent in the Atlantic Ocean whose inhabitants besieged ancient Athens before their homeland sank into the sea. In the mid-1400s, Portuguese mariners kicked off the Age of Exploration by searching the western coast of Africa for the Kingdom of Prester John, a legendary Christian enclave in the heart of the Islamic world, whispered of in Christendom since the days of the First Crusade. Nearly a century later, Spanish conquistadors scoured the jungles of South America for El Dorado, a legendary lost city of gold. Other lost lands include Shambhala, a paradisiacal valley in the Himalayas alluded to in Hindu and Tibetan Buddhist mythology; the Isle of Avalon, the legendary final resting place of King Arthur; and Aztlan, the mythical homeland of the Aztecs.

The Lands of Viking Legend

It might surprise some Canadians to learn that Canada has a few 'lost world' legends of its own. The oldest of these have their roots in the 10th Century Viking voyages to Canada– legendary Norse expeditions immortalized in medieval Icelandic sagas and verified by the ruins of a Viking settlement discovered at the northernmost tip of Newfoundland in 1960.

Helluland, Markland, and Vinland

The Icelandic sagas describe Viking discoveries of three regions west of Greenland. The northernmost of these is *Helluland*, a barren domain of arctic foxes and flat stones which many believe to be the eastern shores of Baffin Island. Below Helluland, Viking mariners discovered *Markland*, a region carpeted with dense evergreen forests filled with wild animals, believed to be northern Labrador. South of Markland, Norse explorers came upon a land abundant with wild grapes, which they called *Vinland*.

Today, historians disagree as to the location of this third region discovered by Viking explorers. Some believe Vinland to be northern Newfoundland, where archaeological evidence indicates a Norse settlement once stood around the turn of the last millennia. Others argue that Vinland must lie further south, perhaps in New Brunswick or New England, where grapes grow naturally in the wild. Others still believe Vinland to be a fabrication intended to attract Viking settlers to a harsher, more northerly colony in the New World.

Land of the One-Footers

In the *Saga of Erik the Red*, the younger of the two Icelandic sagas to chronicle the Norse exploration of the Americas, a party of Viking explorers abandoned their temporary settlement at Vinland after surviving a skirmish with the *Skraelingar*– Vinland's diminutive fur-clad natives. They sailed their longships northwest along North America's Atlantic coast before proceeding up an east-flowing river.

One morning, while camped on the river's northern shore, the Vikings were attacked by a "One-Footer"- a mythical one-legged dwarf which hopped from place to place. Also referred to as "monopods" and "sciapods" by Classical scholars, these characters feature in the writings of the Ancient Greeks and Romans, even appearing in Roman polymath Pliny the Elder's 1st Century encyclopedia *Naturalis Historia*. These agile one-footed monsters were said to abide in India, and their appearance in the *Saga of Erik the Red* might be reflective of a mistaken belief held by the Vikings that Helluland, Markland, and Vinland constituted the eastern shores of the Orient.

The One-Footer hopped up to the Vikings and shot their leader in the lower abdomen with an arrow. The Norseman drew out the projectile and joked that Vinland must be bountiful indeed, as he had grown such a belly that winter that the arrow had failed to harm him. The One-Footer then hopped away to the north, quickly out-distancing the Vikings who pursued him. The Norsemen briefly ventured north into what they assumed must be the land of the One-Footers. Not particularly desirous of another encounter with the little arrow-wielding monsters, however, the explorers soon decided to return to their ship.

Kingdoms of the Skraeling

After spending three more years in the New World, the Vikings sailed for Greenland, their home. *En route*, they stopped in Markland, where they came upon a family of Skraelings consisting of a bearded man, two women, and two children. Although the Norsemen managed to capture the children, the man and the two women disappeared down holes in the earth.

The Vikings adopted the children and taught them their language, Old Norse. The little natives later told their captors that two kings- one of them named Avalldamon, and the other Valldidida- ruled over the land of the Skraeling. The children claimed that their people did not live in houses, but rather dwelled in caves or holes in the earth.

White Man's Land

The native children whom the Vikings captured also alleged that adjacent to their homeland was another territory inhabited by people who dressed in white garments, whose customs included uttering loud cries, carrying long poles, and wearing fringes. The Vikings dubbed this place *Hvitramannaland*, or "White Man's Land".

According to a 14th Century Icelandic manuscript called the *Hauksbok*, the Vikings believed "White Man's Land" to be inhabited by a people called the *Albani*, or "Albinos", whose hair and skin were "as white as snow". Other medieval Icelandic manuscripts, including the *Landnamabok* and the *Saga of the People of Eire*, indicate that the *Albani* were believed to be of Irish Gaelic descent, and that "White Man's Land" was also known as "*Hibernia Major*", or "Great Ireland". Some academics have attempted to draw a connection between the *Albani* and the Papar, the latter being Irish monks who had occupied the Orkney Islands, the Faroe Islands, and Iceland prior to Viking expansion in the Early Middle Ages, and whom some believe fled their remote abodes as a result of pagan persecution. In his controversial 1998 book *The Farfarers: Before the Norse*, Canadian writer and biologist Farley Mowat identified "White Man's Land" as the desolate western coast of Newfoundland, positing that its *Albani* inhabitants were Neolithic Britons who voyaged across the Atlantic thousands of years ago, having been displaced by Celtic tribes.

Today, most historians dismiss the Land of the One-Footers, the Kingdoms of the Skraeling, and White Man's Land as either fictional embellishments resultant of centuries of oral transmission or fables dreamed up by the author of the *Saga of Erik the Red*, the more fantastical of the two Icelandic sagas to describe the Viking voyages to the Americas. A few imaginative scholars have treated the stories seriously and attempted to pinpoint the locations of these lost lands of Viking legend, but none of their theories have gained universal acceptance in the academic community. Unless they are illuminated by new archaeological or historical discoveries, it is likely that the true identities of these lost Viking lands will remain a mystery.

The Lost Kingdom of Saguenay

In 1492, Italian navigator Christopher Columbus rediscovered the New World under the auspices of King Ferdinand II of Aragon and Queen Isabella I of Castile, the rulers of what would soon become a united Spain. Five years later, another Italian navigator named Giovanni Caboto, or John Cabot, sailed west from Bristol, England, in the hope of discovering an alternate route to Asia on behalf of King Henry VII. Instead, he discovered the eastern shores of what was either Newfoundland or Nova Scotia.

A little late to the game, France launched its own New World expeditions in the early 1500s. First, in 1524, an Italian mariner named Giovanni da Verrazano explored the Atlantic seaboard from Florida to Newfoundland, claiming everything between the southern colony of New Spain and the northern English colony of Newfoundland for King Francis I of France. A decade later, Breton mariner Jacques Cartier explored and mapped the Gulf of St. Lawrence on behalf of the same French king, planting a 10-metre-tall wooden cross bearing the words *"Vive la Roi de France"*, or "Long Live the King of France", on the shores of Gaspe Bay near the mouth of the St. Lawrence River.

In the summer of 1534, while erecting that cross, Jacques Cartier and his crew encountered a band of Iroquois Indians who had come to the area for their annual seal hunt. Using sign language, Cartier spoke with the band's chief, Donnacona, and coerced him into allowing two of his sons, named Taignoagny and Dom Agaya, to accompany him across the ocean to France.

During the homeward voyage, Cartier learned from his two Iroquois guests that the village over which their father presided- located at the site of what is now Quebec City- was called a *"kanata"*. Cartier misinterpreted this Iroquois word, which means "village", as a denotation for the entire region, and dubbed the country "Canada".

In May 1535, Jacques Cartier embarked on his second voyage to Canada, equipped with three ships and 110 men and accompanied by the two sons of Chief Donnacona. After a long voyage across the Atlantic, Tainoagny and Dom Agaya led the French explorers across the Gulf of St. Lawrence and up the St. Lawrence River, bound for their father's village, Stadacona. At a point about 190 kilometres (118 miles) downriver from the village, the natives pointed out the mouth of a tributary which emptied into the St. Lawrence on their starboard side (known today as the Saguenay River) and casually remarked that if they travelled west up that river for two days, they would come to the border of a kingdom called Saguenay.

Cartier wrote of the incident in his journal. When translated into English, this entry reads:

"... in the middle of the stream lie three islands, and opposite to them there is a very deep and rapid river, which is the river and route to the kingdom and country of the Saguenay, as we were informed by our two men from Canada. This river issues from between lofty mountains of bare rock with but little soil upon them..."

Cartier's native informants did not elaborate that day on the qualities of this mysterious Kingdom of Saguenay- a domain which would prove in the coming months to be among the most exotic, intriguing, and baffling of Canada's 'lost lands'.

After visiting and exchanging gifts with Donnacona and his band at Stadacona, Cartier and his men, against the chief's advice, continued up the St. Lawrence River in search of another Iroquois village called Hochelaga, to which the chief's sons had alluded during their time in France. Cartier and his crew quickly discovered the village opposite what we now call the Island of Montreal.

The Frenchmen visited Hochelaga and exchanged gifts with the natives. The Iroquois packed a pipe to celebrate the occasion, and thus the explorers became the first Europeans to smoke tobacco.

During the explorers' stay in Hochelaga, the natives pointed to the gold and silver medals that Cartier and his officers wore and explained, using gestures and hand signs, that these metals could be found in great quantities in a land to the northwest- a country occupied by warlike tribes which fought with each other constantly, which could be accessed by the river we know today as the Ottawa. As if to test his informants, Cartier presented them with copper objects and asked if that metal, too, could be found in that mysterious region to the northwest. The Iroquois indicated that the country was not known for its copper, although the metal could be found further to the south.

Could this nameless land of gold and silver, the explorers wondered, have any connection with the mysterious Kingdom of Saguenay?

After concluding their business in Hochelaga, Cartier and his men returned downriver to Stadacona, where they decided to spend the winter. During the cold and bitter months which followed, the Frenchmen learned from their Iroquois hosts that the Kingdom of Saguenay was indeed the same land alluded to by the Hochelaga villagers, said to contain vast quantities of gold and silver. Goaded by their eager French audience, the natives claimed that Saguenay was a vast and populous country whose people dressed in clothing not unlike that worn by the French explorers. Donnacona himself informed the Frenchmen that Saguenay was rich not only in gold and silver, but also in rubies, fine furs, and a large variety of valuable spices, and that its citizens not only wore European-style clothes, but also had white skin, evoking the mysterious "White Man's Land" alluded to in the Viking sagas.

It is interesting to note that, among the many fantastic tales which Donnacona related to the credulous explorers around the campfire that winter was a story echoing the Viking legend of the Land of the One-Footers. "He told us furthermore," Cartier wrote in French, "that he had been... to another country whose inhabitants have only one leg..."

Spring came and Cartier and his men prepared to depart for France. Before leaving, they kidnapped Chief Donnaconna and nine other Iroquois villagers by luring them onto the deck of one of their ships. The explorers pacified the enraged chief by promising him that the King of France would bestow great gifts upon him and his people. With little choice but to submit to the explorers' wishes, Donnacona bid his family farewell as Cartier and his men guided their ships down the St. Lawrence.

The explorers and their indigenous captives arrived safely in France after an uneventful voyage, whereupon Cartier presented the Iroquois chief to King Francis I. In the newly-constructed gallery of the Chateau de Fontainebleau, on the outskirts of Paris, Chief Donnacona regaled the French king with the same tales he had told to Cartier and his men that winter. Foremost among these was the tale of the fabulously wealthy Kingdom of Saguenay, a story in which King Francis I took tremendous interest.

Before the French king had the chance to outfit Cartier for another voyage to Canada, war broke out between France and the powerful House of Habsburg (which controlled both the Spanish and the Holy Roman Empires), the conflict revolving around a dispute regarding control over Northern Italy. Three years after Francis I and Emperor Charles V finally affixed their seals to a truce in 1538, the King of France commissioned Jacques Cartier with leading a third voyage to Canada, this time for the purpose of colonizing New France.

Unfortunately, neither Jacques Cartier nor any of the North American explorers who followed him were able to discover evidence of the mysterious Kingdom of Saguenay. By the end of the 16th Century, even the most imaginative mapmakers, as one historian put it, had "become firmly convinced that Saguenay was a myth, and it disappeared from maps as it had disappeared from the minds of men. It lingered on only in the name of the gloomy river that was supposed to lead to the great empire."

Is there any truth behind the incredible tales that Jacques Cartier and his crew learned from the St. Lawrence Iroquois during their second voyage to Canada?

Maybe, as suggested earlier, the lost kingdom has some sort of connection with the "White Man's Land" alluded to in the Viking sagas.

Perhaps the tale is related to some indigenous memory of the Vikings themselves, who colonized northern Newfoundland and perhaps parts of the Canadian mainland more than five hundred years before Jacques Cartier first set foot in the New World.

Maybe the elusive kingdom was nothing more than a fable invented by Donnacona and the natives of the St. Lawrence for the benefit of their gullible European guests, who were clearly interested in the acquisition of gold and silver.

Or perhaps there truly was an ancient kingdom gilded with gold and rubies hidden away in the wilderness of Quebec, its legacy little more than a fading Iroquois legend by the time of Cartier's first voyage...

The Isle of Demons

In 1541, following his third and final voyage to the New World, Jacques Cartier established a small colony of 400 souls at the site of what would later become Quebec City, not too far from the Iroquois village of Stadacona. This colony, called Fort Charlesbourg-Royal, was the first French attempt at permanent settlement in what would become New France.

Although Cartier and his fellow colonists would abandon the fort two years later on account of harsh weather, scurvy, and incursions by hostile Iroquois warriors, Fort

Charlesbourg-Royal enjoyed a brief tenure as the capital of France's first North American province. King Francis I appointed a French corsair named Jean-Francois de La Rocque de Roberval as Lieutenant General of his new colony, and in the spring of 1542, Roberval set out across the Atlantic, determined to join Cartier and his colonists and assume his position as France's highest-ranking representative in the New World.

The Affair of Marguerite de La Rocque de Roberval

Roberval was accompanied on this voyage by his young unmarried cousin, Marguerite de La Rocque de Roberval. Marguerite caught the eye of a certain French nobleman aboard the ship whose name has been lost to history (although some fictional accounts identify him as Etienne Gosselin, a shipwright), and soon the gentleman began paying visits to young *demoiselle*'s cabin. Encouraged by her servant, an old Norman chambermaid named Damienne, Marguerite began to reciprocate the aristocrat's affections, and in no time the couple were engaging in illicit trysts while Damienne stood watch nearby.

One of the French sailors aboard the vessel discovered the secret affair and reported it to Roberval. Infuriated by his relative's scandalous behavior, the Lieutenant General resolved to maroon his cousin, her lover, and their accomplice, Damienne, on an island off the coast of New France. He rolled out his personal map of the country, which he had acquired from Cartier, and quickly found a place which suited his purpose perfectly- a spit of land with a sinister name, the "Isle of Demons".

The Isle of Demons first appeared in print in 1507, on a famous map of the world drawn by Dutch cartographer Johannes Ruysch, who was an acquaintance and possible shipmate of John Cabot. The isle was said to be large, beautiful, and uninhabited, and natives and whites alike would often hunt and fish on its shores in the daytime. The island's physical charm, however, was but a material façade which served to disguise a dark and frightening secret that lay at its core.

Legend has it that the Isle of Demons was haunted by ghosts and evil spirits, and that if any of its visitors ventured too far into the island's wooded interior, they made themselves vulnerable to its malicious spectral inhabitants. The island's sinister nature was first alluded to in an inscription accompanying Ruysch's 1507 map, which reads, in Latin: "Demons assaulted ships near these islands, which were avoided but not without peril."

According to Andre Thevet, a 16th Century French traveler and Franciscan priest, a number of mariners personally told him that, while passing the island during a storm:

"...they heard in the air, as if on the crow's nest or masts of their vessels... human voices making a great noise, without

their being able to discern intelligible words, only such a murmur as you can hear on market-day in the middle of the public market. These voices caused them a hundred times more astonishment than the tempest around them. They well knew that they were close to the island called the Isle of Demons, but they paid no heed to this fact until some good people offered up prayers and invoked the holy name of Jesus; and little by little the murmur died away, although the storm continued for a long time afterward."

It was on this haunted island that Lieutenant Governor Roberval decided to maroon the hapless trio, leaving them with four aquebuses (matchlock muskets), a quantity of shot and gunpowder, a fire-steel, some provisions, a few iron tools, and a copy of the New Testament.

Resigned to their fate, the castaways decided to make the most of their lamentable situation and set about constructing crude beds and a primitive shelter from spruce boughs. They began to subsist on wild game, which they hunted with their arquebuses, and supplemented their diet with wild fruit.

Each night, the trio was tormented by the island's demons, which assumed hideous forms and capered outside their shelter in the darkness, sometimes shrieking so loudly that, as Thevet put it, "it seemed as if there were more than 100,000 men together."

Weeks turned into months, and soon Marguerite learned that she was pregnant. Unfortunately, her paramour would not live to see the birth of his child. After he succumbed to a fever acquired from consuming contaminated water, Marguerite buried her lover in as deep a grave as she could dig. Her efforts did little to prevent the scent of his decomposing corpse from attracting wild animals, however, and Marguerite found herself spending many an evening driving bears and other scavengers from the noble's tomb with her arquebus.

Unable to withstand the privations of the primitive lifestyle that had been forced upon her, old Damienne passed away before the first snowfall, leaving Marguerite to deliver her child alone. Although both Marguerite and her child survived the birthing, the infant tragically followed her father to the grave shortly thereafter, leaving her mother utterly alone but for the Isle of Demons' eponymous residents.

For nearly three years, Marguerite eked out a living on the accursed island, surviving by her wits and her steadily-dwindling supply of gunpowder. Repenting her sins, she turned to prayer and sacred scripture, spending many hours thumbing through what would become a well-worn Bible. Her prayers were finally answered when, in the autumn of 1544, a crew of Basque fishermen spotted her walking along the shore and rowed over to investigate. After listening to her incredible tale, the fishermen brought Marguerite, along with several bear skins she had preserved (one of them belonging to a polar bear), across the Atlantic to the French city of La Rochelle, where she would later teach reading and writing to the daughters of local noblemen.

Today it is believed that Marguerite and her fellow castaways were marooned on Quirpon Island, a tiny island off Newfoundland's Great Northern Peninsula which bears little resemblance in shape or location to the Isle of Demons which featured so prominently in 16th and 17th Century maps of North America. It appears that Lieutenant Governor Roberval equated Quirpon Island with the sinister-sounding Isle of Demons in an effort to deter future rescue attempts.

If the island on which Marguerite and her companions were stranded was not the real Isle of Demons, then what can account for the diabolical visitors whom Marguerite claimed harassed them at night? Some writers have observed that the sound of the wind whistling through the sea rocks off Quirpon Island has a peculiar humanlike quality, and that great auks- a species of large flightless bird which once thrived in the North Atlantic; which were hunted to extinction in the 19th Century- made truly ghastly noises at night. Perhaps Marguerite's demonic tormentors were little more than the product of this unsettling nocturnal cacophony and an overactive imagination.

If Quirpon Island is truly not the Isle of Demons, then where is that accursed isle located? Despite a once-widespread belief in its existence, the Isle of Demons began to vanish from European maps in the mid-1600s. Today, the Isle of Demons is believed to be a phantom island- a fictional location based more upon travelers' tales than on actual survey work. Perhaps the Isle of Demons is nothing more than a piece of 16th Century fantasy… or perhaps there really is an island in the North Atlantic where demons prowl, waiting for some hapless explorer to venture inland from the island's lonely shores.

The Tropical Valley in the Arctic

Set in Northern Canada in the wake of the Klondike Gold Rush, the fourth and final lost world on this list is far removed from the Atlantic Northeast and the early days of North American colonization. I described this elusive locale in great detail in my book *Legends of the Nahanni Valley*, and thus will restrict my depiction of it here to a few short paragraphs intended to summarize the legend in general.

In 1897, thousands of prospectors from all over the world flocked to the Yukon Territory in northwestern Canada, prompted by news of a gold strike on a tributary of the Klondike River. Few of those who set out for Dawson City, in the heart of the Klondike, actually made it to their destination, and of those few, even fewer managed to strike it rich.

Undaunted, many of those who failed to find their fortunes in Klondike Country searched for gold in other far-flung regions of Northern Canada and Alaska. Throughout the early 1900s, some of these prospectors returned from their boreal wanderings with strange tales of ghosts, phantom lights, and hairy wild men. One of the many incredible tales which made it to the Outside, as northerners often referred to southerly civilization, spoke of a steamy tropical valley in the arctic which remained free of snow and ice through even the most severe winters.

Like the *beyul* of Tibetan Buddhist tradition- Edenic hidden valleys in the Himalayas, said to be protected from snowstorms and wild animals- this arctic oasis was reported to be thick with lush and exotic greenery, kept warm by the many hot springs which ran through it. Despite the huge herds of game which took refuge in this northern paradise, the regional natives who knew of its existence shunned the place, fearful of the evil spirits and huge prehistoric monsters whom they believed inhabited its jungle.

TOP 5 CANADIAN CONSPIRACY THEORIES

WHEN IT COMES TO conspiracy theories, our southern neighbour is undeniably king. Did U.S. Naval Intelligence have advance knowledge of the attack on Pearl Harbor? Was John F. Kennedy really assassinated by a lone gunman? Was the moon landing a hoax? These questions hardly scratch the surface of the bottomless labyrinth of rabbit holes that are America's manifold conspiracy theories.

Although they pale in scope and gravity to those of the United States, the Great White North has a few collusion delusions, sedition suspicions, and connivance contrivances of her own. From the chillingly plausible to the downright absurd, here are five conspiracy theories unique to the land of a maple leaf.

Canadian Conspiracy Theories

1. There's Something in the Coffee

Whether you regularly snag a double-double on your way to work or limit your consumption to RRRoll-Up season, if you're a Canadian java junky, chances are you're intimately familiar with Tim Hortons' coffee. For over half a century, Canada's favourite restaurant has supplied untold road trippers with their caffeine fix, warmed countless frozen fingers at outdoor sporting events, and provided the caffeic catalyst for many a friendly get-together. No doot aboot it, Timmy's coffee is good... some say too good.

Conventional wisdom holds that the popularity of Tim Hortons' iconic beverage is attributable to its rich full-bodied flavour, its reasonable price, and its oft-touted perpetual freshness. According to some, however, that widely-held yet seldom-spoken assumption just doesn't stand up to scrutiny.

Although Tim Hortons undoubtedly makes a solid cup of joe, its brew is objectively far from the finest of its kind. Spend a week indulging exclusively in high-quality coffee from a local roastery and your next cup of Timmy's will probably taste like mud. Yet that very same day, when 5 o'clock rolls around and you fancy an afternoon pick-me-up, it won't be that artisanal coffee you crave...

For some, the only explanation for the irresistible allure of Tim Hortons' coffee is that it contains some sort of ultra-addictive narcotic. Some say that Tim's takes a page out of Coca Cola's old playbook and laces its beans with sprinklings of cocaine. Others whisper that the waxy coating that lines the interior of its paper cups contains trace amounts of nicotine- too little to produce any noticeable effects, but just enough to get you hooked. Whatever the case, many Canucks half-jokingly surmise that there might be more to Tim Hortons' coffee than meets the eye.

2. The NHL is Biased Against Canadian Teams

If there's anything that Canadians love more than Tim Hortons' coffee, it's watching Hockey Night in Canada- a TV program featuring live National Hockey League (NHL) games. Despite Canada's unbridled enthusiasm for its national sport, however, it's been 26 years since a Canadian NHL team won the Stanley Cup, the coveted NHL championship trophy.

There are currently 31 teams in the NHL, and seven of them- namely the Calgary Flames, the Edmonton Oilers, the Montreal Canadiens, the Vancouver Canucks, the Ottawa Senators, the Toronto Maple Leafs, and recently resurrected Winnipeg Jets- are Canadian (the remaining 24 are American).

If the winners of the Stanley Cup were chosen at random, the odds that American NHL teams would win the championship 26 years in a row would be around 1 in 500. Of course, the NHL championship is not a game of chance, and there are many factors which determine a team's likelihood of making and progressing through the playoffs. So what sets Canadian NHL teams apart from their American counterparts?

Are the coaches of Canadian teams less competent than those of American teams? No.

Are the players paid differently? No.

Do American teams have an unfair advantage in the draft? No.

According to some, the only difference between Canadian and American NHL teams is the sort of treatment they receive from the officials during playoffs.

For years, Canadian hockey fans have observed that NHL referees seem to favour American teams, especially during playoff season. Not only do the refs appear to be disproportionately tough on Canadian players- they also seem to turn a blind eye to a staggering number of American infractions. For example, during the third period of 2019's first playoff game between the Boston Bruins and the Toronto Maple Leafs, Toronto's Nazem Kadri was suspended for the remainder of the series for crosschecking Boston's Jake DeBrusk- an incident from which DeBrusk was quick to recover. In game seven of that same series, at a critical moment in the second period when the series was on the line, Boston's Zdeno Chara sucker punched Toronto's captain John Tavares in the side of the head so hard that he fell to the ice... and got away scot free. Hockey fans may recall a similar double standard characterizing this year's playoff series between the Calgary Flames and the Colorado Avalanche.

Why would hockey referees favour American teams over Canadian teams? Some paranoid Canadians suspect that they are pressured to do so by the National Hockey League, which has a financial motive to increase hockey's popularity in the United States. Securing the fanship of America's larger and wealthier pool of sports lovers would certainly allow the NHL to make more money off network revenue. Perhaps, some say, the NHL is doing everything in its power to extend the seasons of American hockey teams for as long as possible in an effort to spread the game throughout the Land of Opportunity.

3. Justin Trudeau is Fidel Castro's Son

Whether your love him or hate him, Canada's Prime Minister Justin Trudeau elicited a universal facepalm across the Western world when he issued his praise-filled eulogy following the death of Cuban dictator Fidel Castro in November 2016. Sure, Justin's father, former Prime Minister Pierre Elliot Trudeau, was a personal friend of the one-time Communist revolutionary, and Justin himself had met with *El Jefe* three months prior to his finis. But haven't the Holodomor, the Cambodian genocide, and the Great Chinese Famine taught leaders of the free world to think twice before showering their dissent-crushing, human-rights-abusing,

Canadian Conspiracy Theories

nuclear-holocaust-flirting Communist counterparts with commendations?

The Prime Minister's baffling public statement prompted many Canadians to take a closer look at Justin's relationship with the late Cuban leader. Almost overnight, a wild theory took form. Perhaps, some said, Justin Trudeau is really not Pierre's son at all, but rather the illegitimate love child of Fidel Castro and Pierre's wife, Margaret.

Immediately, photographs comparing Justin Trudeau with young Castro began to circulate throughout the internet. Take away Fidel's scruffy beard and exchange his combat fatigues for a suit and tie and the resemblance is truly uncanny.

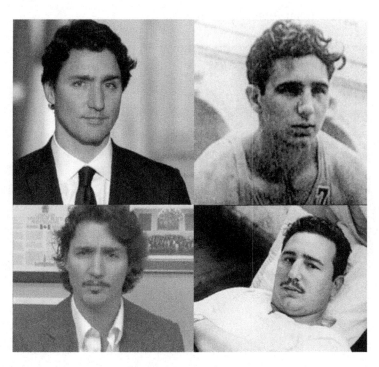

Proponents of the theory noted that both Pierre Trudeau and his wife Margaret, the latter nearly thirty years Pierre's junior, were notoriously promiscuous, and that Fidel became fast friends with Pierre in the 1970s, eventually serving as a pallbearer at his funeral in 2000.

Various fact-checking websites, in response to the rumour, were quick to point out that Justin Trudeau was born on Christmas Day, 1971- five years prior to Pierre and Margaret's famous three-day visit to Havana in January 1976- and that, barring a secret rendezvous, there was no plausible opportunity for the alleged affair to have taken place in the timeframe required for Justin to be *el hijo del Comandante*.

That resemblance, though...

4. Russian Military Jets in Northern Canada

If you've read much of this author's work, chances are that you're familiar with the Nahanni Valley- a mysterious region hugging the junction of the Northwest Territories, Yukon, and British Columbia where, in the early 1900s, prospectors searching for a legendary lost gold mine routinely lost their heads.

Back in the summer of 2018, while interviewing an authority on the Nahanni Valley named Frank Graves, the author of this piece learned of yet another mystery endemic to this infamous vale in Northern Canada. During an expedition to the Nahanni Valley in the summer of 1965, Mr. Graves was informed by the local RCMP that Soviet fighter jets were often seen flying through the region. Frank elaborated on this phenomenon in a contemporary letter to his mentor, Ivan Sanderson, writing:

"Some people- and notably a highly educated white man who has lived in the valley most of his life- remarked to me quite casually one day that enormous airplanes quite often came down from the north and sometimes fly so low in good weather that he could read their large markings even without his binoculars. Besides numbers, they bear 'names' or identifications in the Cyrillic alphabet. Some of these he had tried to copy down, and on showing them to another educated old-timer who had also seen these planes for some years, he learned that a priest from

Ontario had had them translated, and that they were Russian, and standard markings for a certain series of overfly planes known to the Canadian authorities. I have asked around, but I never heard of such planes being spotted anywhere else; so why are the Russians so all-fired interested in this crazy valley? And crazy it is, and in all kinds of ways I later found out..."

Chillingly, recent news suggests that Russian violation of our northern airspace might not be some bygone exercise of the Cold War. Just four months prior to the penning of this piece, on January 26, 2019, U.S. Air Force and R.C.A.F. fighter jets were scrambled to escort two Russian bombers that had ventured too close to Canada's Arctic coast.

5. The Shag Harbour UFO Cover-Up

Speaking of mysterious flying objects, no list of Canadian conspiracy theories would be complete without a nod to the UFO of Shag Harbour, Nova Scotia, and the alleged cover-up surrounding its subsequent investigation by the Canadian military.

On the eve of October 4, 1967, in the tiny fishing village of Shag Harbour on the southwestern tip of Nova Scotia, dozens of witnesses saw an unusual pattern of yellow lights flashing in the night sky. After approaching from the east, the lights hovered over the harbour for some time before plunging down into the water, producing a bright flash of light and a loud boom suggestive of an explosion. Initially fearing that an airplane had crashed into the harbour, several witnesses scrambled to get a better view of the crash site so that they could accurately relay its position to the local authorities. Instead of finding the wreck of a downed aircraft, however, the witnesses met with a strange sight- a pale yellow dome of light floating atop the water's surface. Several young fisherman informed the local Mounties of the incident, and in no time a rescue operation was underway. By the time the R.C.M.P. arrived on the scene, the dome was heading east along the surface of the water, leaving a trail of sparking yellow foam in its wake. The policemen watched as the mysterious object disappeared into the night.

A subsequent Mountie investigation failed to turn up any bodies or debris at the crash site. Suspecting that the mysterious object might have been some sort of secret Soviet military device, the Royal Canadian Navy immediately flew in a team of divers to scour the site for anything out of the ordinary. Like the Mounties before them, the Navy divers were unable to recover anything of interest... at least, that's the official story. Local rumour has it that the Navy divers did recover a component of the mysterious craft on the seafloor, which they wrapped underwater and brought to the surface in secret.

According to UFO researcher Chris Styles, who tracked down and interviewed a number of the divers in the 1990s, one of his informants claimed that the Navy investigation at Shag Harbour was nothing more than a charade conducted for the benefit of the locals and any foreign agents who took an interest in the case. The Canadian military, which diligently monitored the Atlantic Northwest for Russian submarines, knew early on that the mysterious object that crashed in Shag Harbour had actually moved northeast to the waters off Shelburne, Nova Scotia. The Canadian Navy conducted another diving operation near Shelburne, which it kept secret from the public. During this covert retrieval operation, Navy personnel discovered two large crafts underwater, one of which appeared to be lending assistance to the other.

Before the Royal Canadian Navy could conduct a thorough investigation of the crafts, a Soviet submarine entered Canadian waters, apparently in an effort to locate the mysterious objects. While the Canadian cruisers on scene departed to intercept the submarine, the strange crafts slipped away, ascended to the surface, took flight, and disappeared into the sky.

Could there be some truth to the diver's incredible tale? Did the Royal Canadian Navy really cover up evidence of a UFO crash at Shag Harbour, Nova Scotia? Like most great Canadian conspiracy theories, the answers to these questions remain disputed.

THE LEGEND OF OLD WIVES LAKE

OLD WIVES LAKE IS a large saltwater lake located about 30 kilometres southwest of Moose Jaw, Saskatchewan, as the crow flies. Designated a Migratory Bird Sanctuary due to its large seasonal populations of migratory waterfowl and shorebirds, Old Wives Lake is the largest natural lake in southern Saskatchewan and the fourth largest saline lake in North America.

Old Wives Lake owes its peculiar name to an old Cree legend which, as is the case with most oral lore, has a number of different versions. According to one version, which was recounted to the first officers of the North-West Mounted Police by their Metis guides on their Great March West, a Cree hunting party from the east of Wood Mountain (in some versions, the Cree hailed from the Qu'Appelle Valley and travelled southwest via the Fort Qu'Appelle-Wood Mountain Trail) ventured up the Wood River to Old Wives Lake in search of buffalo one spring in the early 1840's.

Earlier that spring, a prairie fire on the eastern plains had decimated the local buffalo population, and the Cree, running low on their winter stores of pemmican, were desperate for food.

Luckily, the Cree discovered a herd of buffalo grazing on the shores of Old Wives Lake. The hunters made camp on the lake's shore and brought down many animals in the ensuing hunt. As the men skinned and dismembered the carcasses, a group of old women, who had accompanied the hunters specifically for this purpose, set about rendering the suet and marrow and drying and pounding the meat to make pemmican. Soon, the Cree had prepared enough food to sustain their starving band back east.

Just as the Cree had finished loading their horses' travois, a Blackfoot war party attacked. Although unprepared, the Cree delivered an effective counterattack and successfully repelled the warriors, who retreated to the nearby hills.

That night, the Cree held a powwow. They knew that the warlike Blackfoot would likely return at dawn in strength, preventing them from returning to their easterly band with the pemmican. After some deliberation, the Cree braves resolved to make a stand and fight, allowing their women and children to escape with the pemmican under the cover of darkness. No sooner had the warriors made their decision, however, than the old wives spoke up. The old wives knew that they, the younger women and the children would

Legend of Old Wives Lake

likely not make it far without the braves, and so they offered to stay behind instead. They had seen many summers, they maintained, and wished to give life to the tribe one last time, as they had in their childbearing youth. The old wives would not be overruled, and so, with great reluctance, the men, women and children of the hunting party left for home with the pemmican in tow.

At the lakeside camp, the old wives tended the fires and talked loudly throughout the night so as to not arouse the suspicions of the Blackfoot. At dawn, a horde of Blackfoot warriors thundered into the camp screaming war whoops. When they discovered that they had been deceived and that the bountiful spoils they had anticipated were reduced to a handful of gray scalps, they tortured and killed the old wives.

Legend has it that the spirits of the dead women haunt a small island in the lake, known as the Isle of Bays, to this day. Some say that on windy spring nights you can hear the old wives' howls of laughter mocking the Blackfoot they deceived.

THE PHENOMENON OF LOST TIME IN CANADA

I WAS BORN IN VANCOUVER, British Columbia, in the summer of 1992, and spent my first four years growing up in the so-called "Rain City". In those days, many American movie and TV production companies shot their films in Vancouver and Toronto instead of Los Angeles or New York City, apparently in an effort to take advantage of the lowly Canadian loonie.

One project which began filming in Vancouver and nearby Squamish, British Columbia, when I was fresh out of the incubator was a TV show called *The X-Files*. This science fiction drama revolves around two FBI special agents named Fox Mulder and Dana Scully, who investigate unsolved cases which invariably involve monsters, aliens, supernatural entities, or some other variety of unexplained phenomena.

Sometime in 2018, my dad informed me that he made an unauthorized (and regrettably invisible) cameo 'appearance' in *The X-Files'* Season 1, Episode 21, entitled

"Tooms". In that episode, the titular Eugene Tooms- a mutant cannibal who subsists on human liver- murdered his psychologist in the house next to my parents'. My dad, while standing in the shadows of his property, watched as Mulder and Scully raced towards the house, guns drawn, in a vain attempt to save the hapless clinician from his unenviable fate.

My dad's confession sparked my own interest in *The X-Files*– an excellent program about which I had previously known next to nothing- and prompted me to binge-watch more episodes than I care to admit. While watching the very first *X-Files* episode, I was introduced to the phenomenon of 'missing time' as an accompaniment to UFO encounters.

In *The X-Files'* pilot episode, while driving on a quiet Oregon highway just outside a town haunted by a series of mysterious deaths, Mulder and Scully are beset by a blinding white light. Their car shuts down and rolls to a stop, whereupon Mulder, who had been looking at his watch when the incident occurred, observes that nine minutes inexplicably elapsed since the flash despite that it seemed to have taken place mere moments before. He then explains to the bewildered Scully that unexplained time loss is frequently reported by UFO abductees.

Betty and Barney Hill's Close Encounter

Indeed, the phenomenon of missing time features in one of the most famous alleged UFO abductions, which took place on the U.S. Route 3 south of Lancaster, New Hampshire, on the night of September 19, 1961. While driving back to their home in Portsmouth, New Hampshire, from a vacation in Niagara Falls and Montreal, couple Barney and Betty Hill claimed to have been approached by a flying pancake-like craft. The strange object followed the couple through Franconia Notch, a pass through the White Mountains, before descending upon them. The Hills heard a series of beeping sounds near the trunk of their car before falling unconscious. Another series of beeping sounds restored the couple to consciousness, whereupon they found that they had travelled 35 miles south down the highway without any memory of the drive. They later learned that they arrived at their home seven hours after their departure from Colebrook, New Hampshire, from which they had begun the final leg of their return journey; the drive from Colebrook to Portsmouth typically takes about three and a half hours.

Subsequently tormented by disturbing dreams, the Hills decided to undergo regression hypnosis in order to determine what exactly took place that night on the highway. During their hypnosis sessions, both Barney and Betty independently recalled being approached by short, grey-skinned humanoids who compelled them to enter their pancake-like craft. The creatures escorted the Hills to separate rooms and told them to lie on rectangular tables before subjecting them to a series of medical tests. When the tests were complete, the creatures returned the Hills to their vehicles and departed into the night sky.

Although Dr. Benjamin Simon of Boston, Massachusetts- the psychiatrist who orchestrated the Hills' hypnosis sessions- concluded that the Hills' recollections were fantasies inspired by some of Betty's dreams, many UFOlogists believe the Hills' testimonies constitute proof that Barney and Betty Hill were abducted by extraterrestrial astronauts.

Ever since the Hills' strange experience, many people have reported similar abductions by the otherworldly occupants of flying saucers. Most of these abduction stories are remarkably similar, one major commonality being the phenomenon of missing time.

The UFO of Verdun, Quebec

Sometime in 2018, my friend and fellow researcher Mr. Gary Mangiacopra introduced me to a UFO sighting published in the October 1952 issue of the magazine *Fate*. The event described, which took place exactly one decade before the Hills' landmark encounter, is remarkable in that it constitutes what might be the first reported incident of lost time in association with UFO sightings in the world.

This brief, somewhat-unintelligible report was submitted by one A.V. Haslett of Verdun, Quebec, a borough of Montreal situated on the banks of the St. Lawrence River.

"One Sunday afternoon in September 1951," Haslett began, "I was fortunate to sight two very bright objects traveling in a southerly direction of the St. Lawrence River, Verdum [sic], Quebec. The first one seemed to be very large and appeared to me like a huge yo-yo with a red band around the middle of it."

Haslett continued:

"I looked at my watch to verify the time in case someone else reported the sighting. The time was 3:42 p.m., and I scanned the sky in case others appeared. Suddenly, another appeared in the same part of the sky and headed in the same direction. This one was either flying higher, or further away, and was the same shape as the first one. I again looked at my watch and was surprised to note that the time was 4:42, exactly an hour after the previous object."

Unless this author has misinterpreted the narrative, Haslett appears to have claimed that an entire hour elapsed between his two UFO sightings in the space of what, in his mind, seemed the blink of an eye. If this is truly the case, then Haslett's story, to the best of this author's knowledge, may be the earliest report of missing time in association with a UFO sighting or alleged alien abductions, Canadian or otherwise.

MIRACLES AND MIRAGES

THE MIRACLE AT LOON LAKE

LAST YEAR'S HOLY WEEK, the week preceding Easter Sunday- was overshadowed by the tragic immolation of Notre-Dame de Paris. On April 15th, 2019, millions of Catholics, Protestants, and Orthodox Christians watched in horror as the vaulted ceiling of that magnificent, 850-year-old symbol of Christendom went up in flames. The structure burned for fifteen hours before collapsing into the nave below, mercifully damaging little of the cathedral's historic interior.

Despite eclipsing it in scale, this disaster eerily echoes the cremation of another house of God by the name of 'Notre Dame' which took place in the Holy Week of 1885, on the northern edge of the Albertan prairies. A savage act of arson, this event played a pivotal role in a series of strange occurrences constituting one of Saskatchewan's least known and most baffling historical mysteries.

1885 was a year of transition in the Canadian West, marking the end of one era and the beginning of another. That fall, the Last Spike of the Canadian Pacific Railway- the iron road connecting the easterly Dominion of Canada with the westerly Province of British Columbia, and bridging the vast North-West Territories that lay in between- was driven home at Craigellachie, B.C. The ringing of the sledgehammer might have served as a summoning bell for hordes of homesteaders who would soon pour into the Canadian prairies, and as a death knell for the days of Canada's brief and fiery Wild West. By 1885, the huge herds of buffalo that had blanketed the prairies since time immemorial had dwindled to near extinction, destined to be replaced in a few short years by their domestic counterparts, beef cattle. The traders, prospectors, and wolfers who, decades prior, had comprised the North-West Territories' only white civilian population had gradually traded in their repeating rifles and revolvers for the lasso of the rancher and the pitchfork of the farmer. And the Blackfoot, Cree, and Assiniboine Indians who had once dominated the region on horseback had been coerced by the Mounties, who brought law and order to the Canadian West in 1874, to abandon the nomadic lifestyle of their ancestors and settle onto Reserves, where their livelihood was reduced to waiting for government rations.

Naturally, there were many who were vigorously opposed to these changes that were swiftly reshaping the face of Western Canada. Foremost among these were the Metis people- the progeny of French-Canadian and Scottish fur traders and First Nations women. Nearly two decades prior, in the wake of Canadian Confederation, the French Metis of the Red River Valley south of Lake Winnipeg had rebelled against the newly-established Canadian government, fearful that Dominion agents would force them to abandon their homesteads along the Red River, which they did not legally own. The uprising, called the Red River Rebellion, was led by a well-educated Metis revolutionary named Louis Riel, who fled south to Dakota Territory when the Canadian government sent a military expedition to enforce peace in the region.

By 1885, the Metis people, who had relied on the bison almost as heavily as their First Nations cousins to the west, were in dire straits. That spring, they invited Riel to return from his long exile in the United States in the hope that he might lead them once again in this their time of need. Answering the call of his people, the Metis expatriate rode north into Canada and up the wagon-rutted Carlton Trail to the village of Duck Lake in what is now Central Saskatchewan, where many Metis had resettled following the Red River Rebellion. In no time, whispers of an impending revolution were rippling throughout the Canadian prairies.

About 300 kilometres (185 miles) northwest of Duck Lake, just west of the eastern border of what is now Alberta, at a place where the southerly prairie meets the boreal forest, lies the remote settlement of Frog Lake. In 1885, this tiny community boasted a grist mill; a Hudson's Bay Company (HBC) trading post; a small North-West Mounted Police (NWMP) barracks and stables; a Catholic Mission church called *Notre Dame du Bon Conseil*, or 'Our Lady of Good Council'; and an office for Indian Agent Thomas Quinn, who was responsible for the three bands of peaceably-inclined Woodland Cree who pitched their teepees nearby.

In the spring of 1885, while Louis Riel was receiving a warm welcome at Duck Lake, two very different Cree bands joined their fellows at Frog Lake. One was comprised of the so-called 'Bush Indians', a peace-loving clan of Woodland Cree who hailed from the forests to the north. The other was composed of fearsome Plains Cree from the southerly prairies who were led by a grizzled, pox-scarred chief named Big Bear.

Big Bear was a true member of the old guard- a man with one moccasin firmly planted in the past and the other begrudgingly thrust into the present. He was the veteran of a thousand skirmishes and horse raids, having spent most of his adult life on the warpath against the Blackfoot, his people's hereditary enemy. He had even played a prominent role in the 1870 Battle of Belly River- the world's last great intertribal Indian battle. Like his ancestors before him, his sole occupations prior to the coming of the Mounties in 1874 had been hunting and warfare- activities which, in his mind, tested his mettle as a chief and defined his worth as a man.

Big Bear detested the changes that had taken place in recent years and stubbornly refused to give up the traditional Plains Cree way of life. Hoping to retain his freedom for as long as possible, he was the last chief to sign Treaty 6- an agreement between the Canadian government and the various Cree and Assiniboine nations of what is now Alberta and

Saskatchewan, which stipulated that the natives surrender their hunting grounds to the government in exchange for provisions. When the buffalo finally disappeared from the prairies and his people began to go hungry, Big Bear had no choice but to accept the terms of the treaty. Instead of settling on a reserve as had his contemporaries, however, the old chief and his band attempted to retain some semblance of their traditional nomadic lifestyle, spending nearly a decade wandering aimlessly from trading post to trading post without any buffalo to pursue. When they finally rode into Frog Lake in the spring of 1885, they were bitter, frustrated, and hungry.

On March 30th, 1885, word reached Frog Lake of a battle which had taken place five days prior at southeasterly Duck Lake. On March 19th, Louis Riel had declared himself the leader of the so-called 'Provisional Government of Saskatchewan'- an independent Metis state comprising much of what is now Alberta, Saskatchewan, and Manitoba. When a handful of North-West Mounted Police officers from Fort Carlton- a Hudson's Bay Company post located about 20 kilometres, or 13 miles, northwest of Duck Lake, on the banks of the North Saskatchewan River- had attempted to make a routine trip to Duck Lake for supplies, Metis revolutionaries had stopped them on the trail and forced them to return with a message from Riel demanding the fort's peaceful surrender. Leif Crozier, the Superintendent of Fort Carlton's NWMP detachment, had no intention of giving in to Riel's demands. On March 25th, he led 95 Mounties down the road to Duck Lake, where 250 Metis revolutionaries were waiting for them, having occupied a defensive position behind several log cabins at the edge of a thicket. Led by their general, Gabriel Dumont, the Metis militia engaged Crozier's force in a thirty-minute firefight which left 12 Mounties and 6 Metis dead. Heavily outnumbered, Crozier had no choice but to retreat to Fort Carlton. And thus Riel and his forces won their first victory in what would come to be known as the North-West Rebellion.

The Plains Cree at Frog Lake were encouraged by news of Riel's success, and almost overnight, Big Bear's son, Imasees, determined to start his own rebellion and fight his way across the prairie to join forces with the Metis malcontents; his father, the old chief, was away on a hunting trip at the time. Eager as he was for an opportunity to change his people's pitiable circumstances, however, Imasees' enthusiasm for the upcoming conflict was eclipsed by that of Wandering Spirit, a hotheaded, curly-haired sub-chief who held more sway over the band's young braves than even Big Bear himself. Wandering Spirit hated white men and blamed them for all the problems the Cree people were currently facing. When Frog Lake's eight Mounties left for Fort Pitt- a Hudson's Bay Company post located 50 kilometres, or 30 miles, southeast, on the banks of the North Saskatchewan- at the request of Frog Lake's white residents, who thought their presence might provoke the Plains Cree to violence, Wandering Spirit decided that the time had come to mete out Indian justice.

Big Bear returned to Frog Lake from his hunting trip on the evening of April 1st, where he learned of Riel's rebellion and of Imasees and Wandering Spirit's desire to take to the warpath. Weary from his journey, the old warrior went to sleep, whereupon Wandering Spirit and his most loyal braves painted their faces with blood red vermillion and yellow ochre before stealing all the horses from the unguarded Mountie stables.

The following morning, at the northwesterly Saint-Charles Mission, situated on the shores of what is now Muriel Lake, something extraordinary happened. This event was recorded by Bishop Vital-Justin Grandin, an Oblate missionary who would take down the statements of the Indian and Metis witnesses to the events of that day about half a year later, in the autumn of 1885. That morning, as the sun peered above the horizon, the prairie sky took on a spectacular gradient of scarlet and crimson as if painted in blood by the hand of God Himself. On this magnificent canvas, the Woodland Cree of Saint-Charles Mission saw nine red crosses hovering in the southeastern sky, in the direction of Frog Lake. The Cree, whose missionary-introduced Catholicism was coloured by the traditional beliefs and superstitions of their ancestors, took this as an omen portending imminent disaster. Under the command of the chief's son-in-law, twenty five of the Muriel Lake Cree grabbed their rifles and set out through the forest in the direction of the heavenly crosses.

Back at Frog Lake, Wandering Spirit and his warriors broke into the homes of the village's white residents and seized their firearms. "Riel and his half-breeds came last night and stole the red coats' horses!" the Plains Cree lied to the bewildered settlers. "But don't be afraid. We will protect you."

After raiding the HBC post of its knives, bullets, and gunpowder, the warriors herded most of Frog Lake's white settlers to the Mission church, where the resident priest, 35-year-old Father Leon-Adelard Fafard, and a visiting priest named Father Marchand, were saying Holy Thursday Mass for the local Metis and Woodland Cree. In the middle of the service, Wandering Spirit sauntered into the church and genuflected in the centre aisle, a Winchester rifle in his hand. According to 23-year-old HBC clerk William Bleasdell Cameron, a witness of the event who described the experience in his 1926 book *Blood Red the Sun*:

"His lynx-skin war-bonnet, from which depended five large eagle plumes, crowned his head; his eyes burned and his hideously-painted face was set in lines of deadly menace. Never shall I forget the feelings his whole appearance and action excited in me as I watched in stupefied amazement while he half-knelt, glaring up at the altar and the white-robed priests in sacrilegious mockery. He was a demon, a wild animal, savage, ruthless, thirsting for blood. I doubted then that we should any of us ever again see the outside of the chapel."

Fathers Fafard and Marchand concluded the Mass prematurely on account of Wandering Spirit's hostile antics, whereupon the war chief's followers ushered most of the white settlers towards the Plains Cree camp. Wandering Spirit himself headed to the home of Thomas Quinn and ordered the Indian agent to follow his white compatriots. Quinn refused. Wandering Spirit repeated his demand twice more, and each time the government man refused to comply. "Die then!" spat the war chief, raising his rifle and shooting Quinn in the head.

The gunshot was like a spark in a powder keg. Immediately, a Plains Cree warrior shot Quinn's Metis interpreter in the shoulder; another pockmarked brave then ran up to the wounded man, pressed the muzzle of his rifle against his chest, and finished him off.

Chief Big Bear, who had been lounging in the kitchen of the HBC post, ran towards the bloody scene bellowing *"Tesqua! Tesqua!"* (Stop! Stop!) in a great booming voice. His entreaty fell on deaf ears; two more white men- William Gilchrist and George Dill- were subsequently murdered by Wandering Spirit's unruly warriors, as were Fathers Fafard and Marchand. A Metis witness named Louis Goulet described the death of Father Marchand in his memoir, writing, "I saw Father Marchand, one of the two priests, fall on his knees, arms crossed, eyes raised to heaven. He was gunned down on the spot. I never saw him move again."

"Dust and smoke filled the air," wrote William Cameron. "Whoops and shrieks and the ghastly clatter of galloping hoofs blended in a weird and ghastly symphony. High over all swelled the deadly war-chant of the Plains

Crees, bursting from a hundred sinewy throats. I heard the peculiarly-ringing voice of Wandering Spirit calling on his followers to shoot the other whites and burst after burst sounded the death knell of other of my friends."

At that time, Theresa Gowanlock, the wife of a local miller named John Gowanlock- was among the crowd of white settlers who were being led to Big Bear's camp. She described her harrowing experience in a later reminiscence entitled *Two Months in the Camp of Big Bear*, writing:

"Mr. Williscraft, an old grey-headed man about seventy-five years of age came running by us, and an Indian shot at him and knocked his hat off, and he turned around and said, 'Oh! Don't shoot! Don't shoot!' But they fired again, and he ran screaming and fell in some bushes."

"My dear wife," whispered Theresa's husband, John, in an attempt to comfort her, "be brave to the end." No sooner had he said this than he was fatally shot in the back. Theresa fell down beside her dying husband and prepared herself for the inevitable bullet. "But death just then was not ordained for me," she wrote. A Plains Cree warrior roughly hauled her to her feet just in time for her to see the murder of John Delaney, who had formerly instructed the local Woodland Cree in farming; Delaney's grieving widow, who was also named Theresa, was torn from her husband's prostrate body and made prisoner.

By the time the smoke cleared, nine white men lay dead and four white residents- Theresa Gowanlock, Theresa Delaney, William Cameron, and HBC agent James Simpson- were held captive in the camp of Big Bear. Cameron and Simpson were spared the slaughter due to the intercession of their Woodland Cree friends, who sheltered them in their own camp after the shooting broke out. Similarly, the two female prisoners, Mrs. Gowanlock and Mrs. Delaney, were saved from cruel usage and death by local Metis interpreters named John Pritchard and Adolphus Nolin, who purchased them from the braves who had claimed them as their wives.

By the time the Woodland Cree from Muriel Lake arrived at Frog Lake, the slaughter was complete. Upon learning the particulars of the massacre, the Indians were certain that the nine red crosses they had seen in the sky that morning were divine memorials for the nine men who had lost their lives that day.

The Plains Cree spent the evening feasting and dancing, gorging themselves on HBC bacon and sacramental wine from the Mission church. After mutilating the bodies of their victims, they allowed several devoutly Catholic local Metis to inter some of the bodies in empty houses and the church cellar; others were left out in the open at the command of Wandering Spirit, at least one of them being propped up against a tree with a pipe jammed in his mouth in a perverse display of frontier humour.

Miracle at Loon Lake

The following day, the natives witnessed a second celestial apparition, which Bishop Grandin described in a letter to the parents of the martyred Father Fafard. From the spire of Notre Dame, two men dressed in white rose up and ascended into the sky, much to the alarm of the natives who were present. As the ghostly figures dissipated, another vision suddenly appeared in the heavens. Witnesses described seeing an altar in the clouds, beside which sat an ethereal priest who seemed to be preparing to say Good Friday Mass. The image dissolved as quickly as it had appeared, leaving many of the Indians in a state of superstitious dread.

On Holy Saturday, Big Bear's Plains Cree burned the Mission church before setting fire to the rest of the buildings at Frog Lake. They whooped and sang as they watched Notre Dame burn to the ground. That accomplished, they and their Woodland Cree brethren, whom they had bullied into joining their wild crusade, made preparations to besiege the southeasterly Fort Pitt.

On Easter Sunday, the Indians held a war council, spending most of the day discussing their next course of action. At nightfall, their camp was beset by a violent thunderstorm. The temperature dropped, and soon a blanket of snow carpeted the prairies. Amidst flashes of lightning, the natives saw another distressing vision in the clouds, which both Bishop Grandin and Theresa Gowanlock described in their writings. While gathered on a hillside near Frog Lake, the natives watched the phantasmal figures of two men rise up from the charred and smoking ruins of Notre Dame, similar to the vision witnessed two days prior. This time, the onlookers recognized the figures as priests. As the spectral forms rose into the air, a cloud suddenly took the form of a church. One of the phantoms entered the church, while the other, who now appeared to be riding a large black horse, held up a cross and made a gesture similar to that which a priest makes when blessing his congregation. Gowanlock, who was asleep at the time of the apparition, wrote that the vaporous priests were described as looking very angry, leading many of the Cree warriors to despair that they had, by their actions, incurred the wrath of God.

For two months, the Cree war party roamed throughout northern Saskatchewan with their prisoners in tow. In their memoirs, Theresa Gowanlock, Theresa Delaney, William Cameron, and Louis Goulet detailed the particulars of the campaign, describing the Cree's nearly bloodless capture of Fort Pitt; the constant infighting that took place between the warlike Plains Cree and their more peaceably inclined Woodland cousins; various Cree ceremonies, including the agonizing Thirst Dance and a ritualized feast which centred around the consumption of dog stew; and the Cree's final skirmishes with government forces at the edge of the boreal forest. All the while, the prisoners- particularly those of the fairer sex- suffered from bitter cold, severe privation, and the ever-looming threat of execution at the hands of Wandering Spirit.

One evening while on the war path, the Plains Cree brutally executed one of their old women, whom Theresa

Gowanlock described as "insane" and William Cameron as "senile". The Indians believed that the woman had been possessed by an evil cannibalistic spirit called a "weetigo", or Wendigo, and that she would try to eat their children if they failed to kill her before sundown. In his memoir, William Cameron implies that the woman was assigned this grim diagnosis on account of her actually expressing a desire to eat human flesh. Similarly, Louis Goulet claimed that "the old lady started ranting and raving in a fever, telling her daughter that if somebody didn't do away with her, she'd turn wendigo after the sun went down." Theresa Gowanlock, however, in a second memoir entitled 'Memories of Frog Lake', written in 1899 shortly prior to her premature death, attributes the woman's death sentence to a different cause. In this piece, which was submitted to the Montreal-based magazine *Family Herald and Weekly Star* by her nephew, Arthur Johnson, and printed in the October 1955 issue of that publication, Gowanlock wrote that the old crone predicted that terrible things would happen to the band as punishment for their murders of Fathers Fafard and Marchand, and implied that the Cree executed her on account of her disturbing prophecies. Whatever the case, Cree warriors brought the woman to the outskirts of the camp, smashed in her skull with a war club, riddled her corpse with bullets, decapitated her, and set her severed head ablaze- an incident which both Cameron and Goulet described in gruesome detail in their memoirs.

Gowanlock described a strange sequel to this ghastly incident in 'Memories of Frog Lake', writing:

"Late in the afternoon some days after this, toward the end of May when we had been captive eight weeks, as Mrs. Delaney and I were inside the lodge, we heard cries of consternation outside. We ran out to see all the band staring in fright at the sky. There in a break among low clouds was a representation of a church resembling that at Frog Lake burned down nearly two months ago with the bodies of the priests and the other white men. As we gazed a priest on a white horse appeared approaching the church. Reaching it he dismounted, stretched out his hand as if in blessing. The summer clouds closed in, and the vision faded away.

"Fear possessed all in the camp. The warning of the murdered old woman was recalled. The squaws, wearied by two months of extra labor of continually moving camp set up a wailing. The warriors had lost the last of their courage. Even the evening meal was untouched. And now the headmen began accusing the young braves of having caused the trouble. The camp did not move again."

Several days later, the disheartened Cree warriors clashed with a combined force of North-West Mounted Police Officers and Canadian militia led by Mountie Sam Steele at the Battles of Frenchmen Butte and Loon Lake. Following their defeat at Loon Lake, the Plains Cree and the Woodland Cree went their separate ways, the prisoners proceeding under the protection of their Woodland Cree friends. The captives were finally rescued by government forces in early June and brought back to civilization.

Miracle at Loon Lake

Most of the surviving perpetrators of the massacre at Frog Lake were eventually captured, although some of them escaped to Montana. On November 27th, 1885, six of the culprits, along with two Cree and Assiniboine murderers from the band of Chief Poundmaker, another participant in Riel's rebellion, were executed at Fort Battleford in what was to be the largest mass hanging in Canadian history. Chief Big Bear himself, who had eluded government forces sent to capture him, eventually turned himself in at Fort Battleford. Due in part to the testimony of William Cameron, who described Big Bear as an unwilling participant in the campaign that was ascribed to him, the great Plains Cree chief was only sentenced to three years of imprisonment.

Although there have been many books and articles written on the subject of the North-West Rebellion, precious few make any reference to the series of spectacular celestial visions allegedly witnessed by the Cree and Metis who participated in Big Bear's campaign. Neither William Cameron nor Louis Goulet made any mention any of the incidents in their memoirs. Even Bishop Grandin, who might have felt inclined to treat the visions as miracles associated with the martyrdom of Fathers Fafard and Marchand, dismissed accounts of the phenomenon as flights of Indian fancy, writing:

"I am convinced that the imagination is for many, if not for all, inherent in all these visions and apparitions. Even those visions which the people of Lac En-Long [Muriel Lake] claimed to have seen cannot be real, if you ask me, but are attributable to

the same cause, since the savages of this locality were ignorant, they assured me, of what had actually happened. All these at least proved the high esteem and veneration which the Christians had for their missionaries, and the remorse felt by the miserable people who had killed them."

Theresa Gowanlock alone gives credence to the stories, strongly implying in her second memoir, which she penned prior to her untimely death, that she herself witnessed the apparition at Loon Lake. Is Gowanlock's 1899 reminiscence the product of the fevered brain of a dying woman- an inadvertent perversion of the events described in her earlier writings? Is it a distortion of the truth written for dramatic effect? Or does it constitute the confession of a troubled soul cognizant of its imminent reunion with its Maker, intended to rectify the omissions of an earlier record born out of a fear of ridicule? Until a more illuminating source emerges from the archives of some Canadian museum or university, these questions will likely remain unanswered, leaving the miracle of Loon Lake one of the great unsolved mysteries of Canada.

THE PHANTOM TRAIN OF MEDICINE HAT

IN THE SPRING OF 1966, columnist Ken Liddell of the Lethbridge Herald interviewed Andrew Staysko, a retired CPR train engineer. Staysko, who had worked for the Canadian Pacific Railway for forty-eight years, told Liddell the strange tale of Medicine Hat's phantom train and the wreck of 1908.

One night in June, 1908, a train departed from the Medicine Hat CPR station, heading east towards the hamlet of Dunmore. The train was to couple with the Spokane Flyer- a deluxe Crowsnest passenger train- in Dunmore and take the former Galt Line west through Lethbridge and down the Crowsnest Line that went into the Crowsnest Pass in the Canadian Rockies. Aboard the train was an engineer named Bob Twohey and a fireman named Gus Day- firemen, or stokers, being the men who shovelled coal into the fireboxes of steam locomotives.

About two miles outside Medicine Hat, the track began to wind around one of the cutbanks surrounding the Ross Creek coulee. No sooner had the train rounded the corner than Twohey and Day found themselves face to face with the headlight of an oncoming train, fast approaching from the east. Instinctively, Twohey dropped his hand to the brake valve, but it was far too late. Before he could crank the lever, however, the approaching train glided laterally off the tracks. Twohey and Day gazed in disbelief as a string of phantom coaches rushed past them.

The spectral crewmembers in the cab waved a greeting to the two horrified trainmen, as CPR crewmembers passing another train would typically do. As Day- who stood weak-kneed in the cab doorway- would later recount, the windows of the coaches that trailed behind the ghostly locomotive were lit. Suddenly, as soon as it had materialized, the phantom train vanished.

Twohey and Day, who both doubted their own senses, remained silent. They continued east without so much as a word, coupled to the Spokane Flyer in Dunmore, and finished their shift without further incident.

In the days to come, Twohey and Day, for the most part, kept their strange tale to themselves. Gus Day, after some time, began to relax and wrote off the incident off as an experience of life. Bob Twohey, on the other hand, feared that the phantom train was a premonition portending something terrible. Unable to get the thought out of his mind, he sought

Phantom Train of Medicine Hat

the advice of a fortune teller. Sure enough, the fortune teller predicted that Twohey would die within the month.

About two weeks after their incident with the phantom train, Twohey and Day met on a street in Medicine Hat. Perhaps feeling safer with the passage of time, the two trainmen found the courage to ask each other what they had seen that strange night. To their immense relief, they found their accounts to be identical.

Twohey told Day about the fortune teller's prediction, and that he planned to lay off for a couple of trips. Following their conversation, he booked some time off and went to stay with some relatives in the city of Lethbridge, Alberta. Day, on the other hand, stayed on the job.

A few nights later, Day was assigned a job nearly identical to the one which he and Twohey had worked on that strange night. In the exact same engine, Day was to travel east from the station, couple with the Spokane Flyer in Dunmore, and proceed west to the Crowsnest Pass. This time, however, the engineer working the shift was a man named J. Nicholson.

That night, just as the engine rounded a corner in the Ross Creek coulee, the phantom train appeared again with the whistle blowing and the headlight glowing. Just as before, the train sped past on invisible parallel tracks, with the ghostly crewmembers waving greetings from their positions in the cab and the cars. Before poor J. Nicholson knew what was happening, the train disappeared into the dry prairie air.

On the morning of July 8th, 1908, J. Nicholson boarded the same locomotive that he had operated with Day several nights earlier (the night on which he witnessed the ghost train). He was accompanied by H. Thompson, a fireman; Gus Day, who was usually the fireman on that locomotive, had been assigned to yard service. Just as before, the locomotive was scheduled to travel east to Dunmore, couple with the Spokane Flyer, and head west into the Crowsnest Pass.

When the train was about 100 yards from the location on which the phantom train had been spotted on two different nights, another train appeared around the bend. This time, however, it was daylight, and it was for real. The oncoming train was the No. 514 passenger train from Lethbridge, and the engineer at the throttle was none other than Bob Twohey, who had overcome his fears and returned to work.

In the ensuing crash, both engineers, Twohey and Nicholson, died on impact. A fireman named Gray and a conductor named Mallet, both crewmembers of the inbound passenger train, along with seven of the passengers, were also killed in the crash. H. Thompson, the Medicine Hat fireman, leapt from the cab just in time.

More Miracles and Mirages

In the months following my online publication of this article, I received comments from two different Albertan gentlemen who had experienced strange phenomena of which this piece reminded them, and which they suspected might be connected in some way to the tale of the phantom train. The first of the comments, submitted by Mr. Ray Bosch, reads:

"I can't believe what I just read, because one week ago, during a severe rain storm, we- my wife and I- were awakened by a sound that sounded like a train, and thought a tornado was coming, as we were told that a tornado sounds like a train.

"We live on an acreage south of Medicine Hat, with train tracks close to our home. At approximately 1:00 A.M., we both looked out our window and saw a train all lit up, going east towards Dunmore. All the boxcars were clear and brightly-lit, every one of them. We could not comprehend what we had seen, as we had never seen a train lit up like that before. Also, we did not hear a whistle blow as they usually do when they cross 13th Avenue... very odd.

"I told my daughter, and she showed us this website, and the story of the phantom train of Medicine Hat. I am amazed, excited, and fearful at the same time. What is this all about? Why did we see it? What does it mean?"

The second gentleman to comment on my article, Mr. Brian Gale, wrote the following:

"In the late 1970's, I drove a school bus on the Black and White Trail that crosses the train line to Lethbridge just before the train intersection that goes to Medicine Hat on the left and Dunmore on the right. As a bus driver, you had to stop before the train tracks and open your door and listen for a train. One day, I stopped at the tracks and looked around, and off in the distance was housing from the Taylor subdivision part of Ross Glen [located at the same place in which the phantom train story is set]. The thing was that the Taylor neighbourhood wasn't built until about five to seven years after this, but that day, I could see it plain as day..."

NAUTICAL MYSTERIES OF CANADA'S GREAT LAKES

FOR CENTURIES, North America's five Great Lakes have served as the setting for a host of legends, folktales, and nautical mysteries. The local Ojibwa First Nations, for example, tell stories of fabulous monsters which inhabit the depths, shores, and skies of these inland seas, from the *Mishipeshu*, a huge horned aquatic creature imbued with mystical powers; to the Thunderbird, the enemy of the *Mishipeshu*, responsible for the creation of lightning storms; to the *Memogovissiouis*– long-haired sirens who reside within the coldest, deepest recesses of these freshwater oceans. French-Canadian voyageurs who paddled their birch-bark canoes across these waters during the days of the North American fur trade had their own tales of haunted spots and curious locales, like the Pictured Rocks on the shores of Lake Superior– a series of colourful sandstone bluffs pitted with dark caverns which were said to be home to the mischievous spirit of the Ojibwa's legendary patriarch, whom the French called *Menni-boujou*; and *La Cloche*– a strange rock on an island in Lake Huron which, when struck, rang like a bell across the water. More modern Michigan lore is replete with stories of bottomless subterranean outlets which connect these massive bodies of water with smaller adjacent lakes and waterways. Legend has it that underwater currents draw the corpses of drowned fishermen into these outlets, engendering another popular folktale which contends that the Great Lakes never give up their dead.

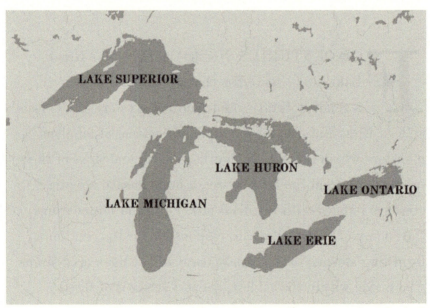

The Wreck of the Edmund Fitzgerald

Of all the strange stories and legends surrounding the Great Lakes, perhaps the most chilling are those pertaining to the host of ships and sailors whom the Lakes have swallowed over the years. Undoubtedly, the most famous of these is the tale of the SS *Edmund Fitzgerald*, a massive Great Lakes freighter whose mysterious and untimely demise was immortalized in Canadian folksinger Gordon Lightfoot's 1976 hit song "The Wreck of the *Edmund Fitzgerald*".

The story of the SS *Edmund Fitzgerald* begins in 1957, when an American insurance company called Northwestern Mutual commissioned the ship's construction and named it after its president. With a length of 729 feet (222 metres) and a gross registered tonnage of 13,632, it was, at the time of its launch, the largest vessel to ever ply the waters of the Great Lakes.

The SS *Edmund Fitzgerald* began its career on an ominous note. During its christening in Detroit, Michigan, Elizabeth Fitzgerald, the wife of the businessman after whom the freighter was named, tried three times to smash a champagne bottle over the ship's bow, succeeding only on the last. When the ropes securing the ship to the shore were subsequently severed, the freighter slid down a ramp into the Detroit River and hit the water at an awkward angle, sending up an enormous wave that doused all who attended the ceremony. The shock of the cold water sent one of the onlookers into cardiac arrest; the fifty-eight-year-old attendee, who had travelled from Toledo, Ohio, to witness the launch, died on the scene.

Despite its inauspicious inauguration, the SS *Edmund Fitzgerald* went on to enjoy a brief but prosperous career hauling taconite (processed pellets of iron ore) across the Great Lakes. Due to its speed and cargo capacity, the freighter routinely set hauling records during the 748 trips it completed throughout its lifetime.

On the afternoon of November 9, 1975, the SS Edmund Fitzgerald left Superior, Wisconsin, for a steel mill near Detroit, its cargo hold filled with 26,000 tons of taconite. She was captained by Ernest McSorley, a heavy-weather Canadian-born mariner known for his quiet stoicism and his willingness to sail through rough waters, and was crewed by 28 veteran sailors. About three hours into her voyage, she overtook and was subsequently trailed by another taconite-laden cargo ship called the SS *Arthur M. Anderson* whose captain, Jesse "Bernie" Cooper, agreed to accompany the *Edmund Fitzgerald* across Lake Superior.

At that time, a winter severe storm was making its way across the lake. Fueled by the collision of cold Arctic winds with warm fronts from the Gulf of Mexico, these ferocious cyclonic gales are referred to colloquially as the "Witch of November". Trusting in the experience of their crews and the integrity of the vessels they commanded, neither McSorley nor Cooper thought twice about steering their freighters into the heart of this rapidly-intensifying tempest.

The prudent captains adopted a course along Lake Superior's northern Canadian shore, which would offer them some protection from the storm, and kept in regular contact with each other via radio. The *Edmund Fitzgerald* and the *Arthur M. Anderson* pushed on throughout the night, weathering what Captain McSorley described as "the worst sea [he had] ever been in". The freighters were whipped by 60-mile-per-hour winds and battered by ten-foot-tall waves which gradually wore down the *Edmund Fitzgerald*. By 3:30 A.M., the freighter had begun to lean to one side. By 5:30, the ship had lost both its radars to the wind and was taking heavy waves over her decks.

At 7:10 that evening, when the *Edmund Fitzgerald* was about fifteen nautical miles from Whitefish Bay and the twin cities of Sault Ste. Marie beyond, Captain Cooper's first mate, Morgan Clark, radioed Captain McSorley to inform him of the presence of a ship which lay ahead of him. He concluded the transmission by asking how the *Edmund Fitzgerald* was faring. "We're holding our own," was McSorley's reply.

That was the last anyone ever heard from Ernest McSorley or his crew. Mere moments later, the *Edmund Fitzgerald* suddenly and mysteriously plummeted 530 feet down to the bottom of Lake Superior, twisting in half in the process and entombing Captain McSorley and his crew of 28 in a frigid watery grave. There were no witnesses of the disaster; the crew members of the *Arthur M. Anderson* only realized that something was amiss when McSorey failed to respond to their radio queries and when they found that they were unable to see any of the *Edmund Fitzgerald's* lights in the distance when the fog cleared.

When the enormous freighter failed to appear on his radar screen, Captain Cooper called the Canadian Coastguard and informed them of the situation. An hour later, the American and Canadian Coast Guards launched a joint aerial search for the missing vessel and its crew. The rescue team's efforts were soon supplemented by those of the crews of the *Arthur M. Anderson* and the *William Clay Ford*, the latter a freighter anchored nearby, which left the relative safety of Whitefish Bay and joined the search for the *Edmund Fitzgerald*. Despite a thorough and concerted search, the only trace of the freighter that the rescue team managed to find that day were the remains of a lifeboat shattered beyond repair.

The following day, as news of the missing freighter began to circulate throughout the Great Lakes region, Father Richard Ingalls of the Mariner's Church of Detroit rang his church's bell 29 times, each toll representing a lost crewmember of the *Edmund Fitzgerald*. For thirty one years, the reverend of the Mariner's Church would continue to perform this ritual on the anniversary of the freighter's disappearance, afterwards altering the ceremony so that it honoured all the sailors who have lost their lives on the Great Lakes throughout the years.

Three days later, a U.S. Navy aircraft equipped with a metal detection device discovered the wrecked SS *Edmund Fitzgerald* lying in two pieces at the bottom of Lake Superior about fifteen nautical miles from the mouth of Whitefish Bay. Subsequent diving operations, one of them conducted by marine explorer Jean-Michel Cousteau (the son of the celebrated French explorer Jacques Cousteau), failed to recover any of the bodies of the 29 sailors who went down with the ship.

Throughout the next two decades, many different theories were put forth as to the cause of the freighter's demise. Some believed that the *Edmund Fitzgerald* had sustained fatal damage while bottoming out on the Six Fathom Shoal northwest of Caribou Island, not far from its final destination. Others maintained that the freighter had been buried by twin rogue waves measuring about 35 feet in height, which the crew of the Arthur M. Anderson had encountered at 6:40 P.M. on the evening of November 10th. Others still suggested that the ship's cargo hold was flooded due to the crew's failure to properly close the hatches that sealed it from the elements. To date, authorities disagree on the specific factors which contributed to the sinking of the *Edmund Fitzgerald,* and to this day, the true cause of the freighter's capsizal remains one of the greatest unsolved mysteries of the Great Lakes.

In the summer of 1995, Canadian explorer Dr. Joseph B. MacInnes led a series of dives on the sunken ship, during which he salvaged the freighter's bell- an artifact which some writers have described as the symbolic heart of the ship. MacInnes later replaced the bell with a replica on which was inscribed the names of the 29 sailors who went down with the freighter- a headstone marking the final resting place of the sailors who lie forever within the wreck of the *Edmund Fitzgerald.*

Le Griffon

Although the SS *Edmund Fitzgerald* was the largest ship ever claimed by the Great Lakes, she was neither the first nor the only. Over the past four centuries, over 6,000 ships have come to rest beneath the waves of these five inland seas. Notwithstanding the scores of native birch bark canoes and French bateaus which must have foundered in these freshwater oceans in centuries past, the first real ship to disappear in the Great Lakes was a French barque called *Le Griffon*, or "The Griffon".

Le Griffon was constructed in the year 1679 by Rene-Robert Cavelier, Sieur de La Salle, an ambitious French adventurer remembered today for his establishment of a vast bygone province known as French Louisiana. Trained in France as a Jesuit priest, La Salle left the Jesuit Order in 1667 to pursue fame and fortune in Canada- at that time, a French colony called New France. After acquiring some land on the Island of Montreal, he had led an unsuccessful expedition in search of the Northwest Passage- the legendary waterway through North America connecting the Atlantic with the Pacific. In 1672, he allied himself with Louis de Buade, Compte de Frontenac, the newly-appointed Governor of New France. Frontenac hoped to expand the colony westward from its confines in the valley in the St. Lawrence River and bring the fur trade to the Great Lakes- a wild region populated at that time by warring native tribes, a handful of Jesuit missionaries, and independent fur traders called *coureurs des bois*, or "runners of the woods". In 1673, La

Salle helped the Governor establish Fort Frontenac at the junction of the St. Lawrence and Lake Ontario- the colony's first real incursion into the Great Lakes.

In 1677, La Salle sailed to France for the purpose of convincing King Louis XIV to grant him permission to establish two more forts on the Great Lakes- one of them at the mouth of the Niagara River, and the other at the southern end of Lake Michigan. He also requested a license to build a sailing ship on Lake Erie, at the end of the Niagara River opposite Lake Ontario. The king granted his request, and La Salle sailed for Canada with thirty shipwrights, carpenters, blacksmiths, and soldiers, as well as an abundance of supplies.

La Salle began his enterprise by splitting his party into three groups. One disembarked in canoes and paddled ahead to Lake Michigan to establish a trading relationship with the natives there. Another, headed by a Recollect friar named Father Louis Hennepin and a French Royal Army officer named Dominique la Motte de Luciere, set out in a small sailing vessel for the Niagara River, where they were to choose the location of a new fort. La Salle himself, accompanied by a French maritime pilot and a one-handed Italian soldier named Henri de Tonti, took a small sailing ship to a native village on the shores of Lake Ontario to secure winter provisions for his crew.

The enterprise began with a rocky start. Unbeknownst to La Salle, most of the men sent to Lake Michigan squandered their trade goods and deserted. The ship headed by Hennepin and La Motte became encased in ice near present-day Toronto, and had to be liberated with axes before its occupants could make their way across Lake Ontario to the mouth of the Niagara River. And although La Salle and Tonti managed to obtain provisions at a native village, they lost everything in an accident on Lake Ontario.

The party headed by Hennepin and La Motte managed to reach the mouth of the Niagara River and choose a suitable building site for the fort, which was to be named 'Fort Conti' after one of La Salle's aristocratic Parisian friends. A few of them decided to head further up the river to the base of what is now Queenston Heights. Excepting, perhaps, a few earlier Jesuit missionaries who failed to write about the experience, Hennepin and his companions thus became the first white men to see the Niagara Falls.

That accomplished, Hennepin, La Motte, and company struck out westward through the forest to a newly-established

Seneca Iroquois village, where they hoped to have their enterprise sanctioned by the local chief. Back in the 1640s and '50s, the warlike Iroquois Confederacy had left their haunts in the forests of upstate New York to launch a massive offensive against the Huron, Erie, Neutral, and Petun Nations of the Great Lakes. Armed with muskets and steel tomahawks supplied by their Dutch and English allies to the southeast, they wiped out entire nations and drove others from their traditional hunting grounds. In the 1660s, the colonists of New France found themselves drawn into the conflict, obliged to defend their allies from the Iroquois invaders. After a series of bloody skirmishes and counteroffensives, New France made a tentative peace with the Iroquois Confederacy in 1666, allowing the invaders to settle the lands of the First Nations they had conquered. Ever since, a shaky tranquility had reigned over the eastern Great Lakes. Eager to maintain the status quo, Hennepin and La Motte were dismayed when the Seneca chief failed to give his blessing to their enterprise.

Fortunately, La Salle had better luck than his subordinates. Upon arriving from his misadventure on Lake Ontario, the explorer personally paid a visit to the chief and convinced him that the Iroquois would benefit from their undertaking. Finally, with the chief's tentative approval, the Frenchmen commenced the construction of Fort Conti. In addition to the fort, they also began building a 45-ton barque, or sailing ship, above the Niagara Falls.

The construction of this vessel was an unpleasant task for La Salle's men, who began the project by hauling deck spikes, rigging, and other equipment up the portage trail to the riverbank above Niagara Falls. Throughout the winter, spring, and early summer, they labored with frozen fingers and empty stomachs, all the while wary of the sullen Iroquois braves who often loitered around the worksite, fingering their tomahawks and war clubs. While his men worked on the ship and the fort, La Salle himself, accompanied by two of his employees, travelled by snowshoe through the forest and across Lake Ontario to Fort Frontenac, where he hoped to replenish the provisions he had lost in the lake.

During La Salle's absence, the men on the Niagara River completed both the fort and the 45-ton ship. The latter was christened *Le Griffon*, or "The Griffon", that mythical monster being the primary ornament on Count Frontenac's coat of arms. Its prow bore a wooden carving of the legendary half-lion/half-eagle for which it was named, and its decks bristled with seven small cannons which were fired at its christening.

La Salle finally returned to the Niagara River in early August, this time accompanied by three Flemish friars. Eager to make use of the new ship, he and all his men embarked on *Le Griffon* and set out on her maiden voyage across Lake Erie.

For three days, the explorers sailed down the length of the lake. On the fourth day, they turned north and sailed up the Detroit River. They crossed Lake St. Clair beyond and proceeded up the St. Clair River into Lake Huron. There, the explorers were beset by a ferocious gale which threatened to capsize their vessel. Praying to St. Anthony of Padua, the patron saint of mariners, the sailors managed to make their way up Lake Huron to the Island of Michilimackinac, home to Indian villages and a Jesuit mission, and a haven for *coureurs des bois*.

La Salle and his crew received a cool welcome from the Jesuits, in whose chapel they celebrated Mass. The explorers were also greeted by the local Huron and Ottawa Indians who were amazed at the size of their ship. During their visit, they received the disheartening news that most of the fifteen men whom La Salle had previously sent to establish a trading relationship with the Indians of Lake Michigan had squandered his trading goods and abandoned their mission.

In early September, La Salle and the crew of *Le Griffon* sailed west from Michilimackinac into Lake Michigan and further southwest into Green Bay. There, on an island, he found the few members of his advance party who had remained loyal to him, discovering to his pleasure that they had acquired a small fortune in furs from their trade with the natives. La Salle then had these furs loaded into the cargo hold of *Le Griffon* and ordered a handful of his men to transport them to Fort Conti, asking the ship's pilot to return to Lake Michigan as soon as the cargo was unloaded. *Le Griffon* departed on September 18th, 1679, just as a storm began to brew.

Aside from the vessel's own crew, La Salle and his explorers were the last men to set eyes on *Le Griffon*. The vessel disappeared on her homeward voyage somewhere in the waters of Lakes Michigan, Huron, or Erie. Most assumed that the ship had foundered in a storm and was lost with all hands. This theory is supported by the discoveries of Albert Cullis, who manned the Mississagi Strait Lighthouse on Manitoulin Island in the 19th Century; in the late 1890s, Cullis reputedly discovered a watch chain, three 17th Century coins, and five human skeletons in and around a cave on Manitoulin Island. Another theory regarding the fate of *Le Griffon* contends that the ship was boarded by hostile Indians who murdered her crew before setting her ablaze; La Salle and his crew certainly had their fair share of rivals who would stop at nothing to protect their own interests in the fur trade. La Salle himself suspected that the ship's occupants had intentionally scuttled *Le Griffon* and made off with the furs she contained; in letters to Count Frontenac, the explorer wrote about an Indian rumour which held that, in 1680, white men matching the description of the crew of *Le Griffon* had been captured by Indians on the Mississippi River paddling canoes filled with valuable goods. The natives killed every crew member but the captain, whom they took prisoner. La Salle believed that these unfortunates constituted his ship's crew, who had intentionally sunk his vessel and made off with his furs, intending to join a famous *coureurs des bois* named Daniel Greysolon, Sieur du Lhut. Whatever the case, *Le Griffon's* undiscovered wreck is considered today to be the Holy Grail of Great Lakes shipwreck hunters.

The *Hamilton* and the *Scourge*

Over a hundred and thirty years after *Le Griffon's* disappearance, half a century after France ceded Canada to Great Britain and nearly four decades after Britain ceded her Thirteen Colonies to the United States, the Great Lakes resounded with the thunder of cannons and the rattle of musketry in a conflict known today as the War of 1812.

Angered by the British Royal Navy's practice of impressing American citizens into service, and insulted by King George III's attempts to prevent American merchants from trading with Napoleonic France, with whom Britain was at war, the United States Congress declared war on Great Britain, initiating the War of 1812. Throughout the summer and autumn of that year, the Great Lakes bore witness to a number of deadly clashes between American and British-Canadian forces, including the successful British Siege of Detroit and a failed American invasion of Upper Canada- the Canadian side of the Great Lakes.

On April 27, 1813, the U.S. Army and Navy launched an attack on the British city of York (present-day Toronto), situated on the western shores of Lake Ontario. The American soldiers successfully captured the city, only to be killed and maimed by the detonation of the fort's powder magazine, this tremendous explosion having been orchestrated by the retreating British. The Americans avenged this act by plundering the town and setting many of its buildings on fire.

The U.S. troops went on to attack and capture the southeasterly Fort George, situated at the mouth of the Niagara River. Later that summer, they attempted to besiege a British garrison at present-day Burlington, Ontario, southwest of York. The British Royal Navy sailed out to stop them, and thus, on the morning of August 7th, 1813, the British and American Great Lakes fleets found themselves face to face, just beyond cannon range of one another, unable to engage due to an uncharacteristic absence of wind which settled over Lake Ontario.

One of the vessels in the U.S. fleet during this spell was a Canadian merchant schooner-turned-American war ship called the USS *Scourge*, and one of the sailors aboard that vessel was a Canadian expat named Ned Myers. Many years later, Myers would tell his story to celebrated American novelist James Fennimore Cooper, who put his tale into print in his 1843 biography of him entitled *Life Before the Mast*. Myers, via Cooper's book, wrote:

"It was a lovely evening, not a cloud visible, and the lake being as smooth as a looking-glass. The English fleet was but a short distance to the northward of us; so near, indeed, that we could almost count their ports. They were becalmed, like ourselves, and a little scattered."

After having their supper, Myers and the crew of the USS *Scourge* bedded down next to the cannons. Myers wrote:

"I was soon asleep, as if lying in the bed of a king. How long my nap lasted, or what took place in the interval, I cannot say. I awoke, however, in consequence of large drops of rain falling on my face... When I opened my eyes, it was so dark I could not see the length of the deck..."

As Myers snuck away from his post to retrieve a bottle of grog, the schooner on which he served was suddenly beset by a violent storm. The *Scourge* quickly took on water and, in less than a minute, began to sink.

"The flashes of lightning were incessant, and nearly blinded me. Our decks seemed on fire, and yet I could see nothing. I heard no hail, no order, no call; but the schooner was filled with the shrieks and cries of the men to leeward, who were lying jammed under the guns, shot-boxes, shot and other heavy things that had gone down as the vessel fell over...

"I now crawled aft, on the upper side of the bulwarks, amid a most awful and infernal din of thunder, and shrieks, and dazzling flashes of lightning; the wind blowing all the while like a tornado... It now came across me that if the schooner should right, she was filled, and must go down, and that she might carry me with her in the suction. I made a spring, therefore, and fell into the water several feet from the place where I had stood. It is my opinion the schooner sank as I left her."

Myers began to swim for the first time in his life. By chance, he bumped into a lifeboat, into which he managed to climb. Through an oppressive darkness punctuated by blinding flashes of lightning, he searched for survivors and managed to drag seven fellow soldiers into the tiny craft. Myers and his shipmates were later rescued by American sailors whose ship had survived the tempest.

In addition to the *Scourge*, the storm claimed another U.S. Navy schooner called the USS *Hamilton*. Of the 102 sailors aboard these vessels at the time of the squall, only sixteen survived their capsizing, many of them having been trapped inside the ships during their 300-foot descent to the bottom of the lake.

Legend has it that on foggy nights in the waters outside Burlington, Ontario, sailors sometimes spy two old-fashioned square-sailed vessels, with their gun ports open and their decks illuminated by the eerie glow of lanterns hanging in the rigging. As soon as they are spotted, these phantasmal vessels shake as if buffeted by unearthly winds before sinking beneath the surface, all the while accompanied by the faint shrieks of drowning sailors whose skeletons lie below, entombed within the wrecks of the USS *Scourge* and the USS *Hamilton*.

Old Whitey and the Ghosts of the SS *Kamloops*

Another of the thousands of ships devoured by the Great Lakes over the past four centuries is the SS *Kamloops*, a steam-powered freighter which sank in 1927 with all hands off Isle Royale in Lake Superior just south of Thunder Bay, Ontario. What distinguishes the SS *Kamloops* from other Great Lakes wrecks are the crewmembers, both corporeal and ethereal, who are said to still wander its decks at the bottom of the lake.

The SS *Kamloops* began her life in 1924, in a shipyard in North East England. Commissioned by the Montreal-based shipping company Canada Steamship Lines, she had a length of 250 feet and a gross tonnage of 2,402, making her one of the smaller freighters on the Great Lakes at that time. Her limited size allowed her to traverse the Welland Canal, an artificial waterway connecting Lake Ontario with Lake Erie.

After steaming across the Atlantic Ocean and up the St. Lawrence River to her home on the Great Lakes, the SS *Kamloops* was put to work hauling manufactured goods, many of them destined for the rapidly-developing Prairie Provinces, from the St. Lawrence to Lake Superior. Due to the hazardous Great Lakes freighting practice of shipping as late as possible prior to winter freeze-up, the steamer and her crew had a few close calls. In 1926, for example, the freighter became trapped in ice in the St. Mary's River, the waterway which connects Lake Huron with Lake Superior.

In late November, 1927, the SS *Kamloops,* under the command of Captain William Brian, was tasked with hauling a mixed cargo from Montreal to Fort William, Ontario- a district of what is now Thunder Bay. On this journey, it trailed the wake of the SS *Quedoc*, an empty grain carrier also bound for Fort William. The *Kamloops* passed through the Soo Locks, a water lift on the St. Mary's River, on December 4th, when it was beset by a howling northern gale.

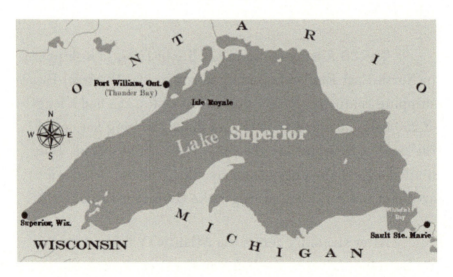

On the night of December 6th, in the waters off Isle Royale, the captain of the SS *Quedoc* spied a dark misshapen mass looming before him through the fog. He and his crew frantically manoeuvered their vessel to avoid the mysterious obstacle and narrowly avoided what promised to be catastrophic collision. They sounded their foghorn to warn Captain Brian and the crew of the *Kamloops* and continued on to Fort William. Disturbingly, the SS *Kamloops* failed to make it into port that night.

In the days that followed the storm, search and rescue crews scoured the surrounding area for a number of different ships that had failed to arrive at their destinations. Most of these were found stranded in different areas of the lake, having been blown off course during the gale. Only the SS *Kamloops* remained unaccounted for.

Canadian winter descended upon the Great Lakes shortly after the freighter's disappearance and the waters of Superior began to freeze. It soon became apparent to even the most hopeful friends and family members that there was virtually no chance that any of the SS *Kamloops'* crew of twenty-two had survived the mysterious calamity that had befallen their ship.

In the spring of 1928, fishermen plying their trade off the coast of Isle Royale discovered two half-frozen corpses washed up on the island's shore. The bodies were identified as crew members of the SS *Kamloops*. Several months later, in early June, fishermen found six more bodies on the island, five of them huddled together as if for warmth. One of the corpses was identified as 22-year-old Alice Bettridge, one of the two women serving aboard the SS *Kamloops* on the night of its disappearance. Half a year later, a trapper discovered a handwritten note in a pickle jar near the mouth of the Agawa River, across Lake Superior from Isle Royale, which Alice had apparently scrawled in her final moments. The message reads,

"I am the last one left alive, freezing and starving to death on Isle Royale. I just want mom and dad to know my fate." The letter was signed, "Al, who is dead."

On August 21st, 1977, Minneapolis-based recreational diver Ken Engelbrecht discovered the wreck of the SS *Kamloops* while searching for the vessel off the northern shore of Isle Royale. The steamboat lay on her starboard side 270 feet below the water's surface. Inside the ship's engine room floated two human corpses with snow-white skin, both of them in excellent condition due to the preservative effects of the ice-cold water in which they were immersed and the relative absence of aquatic life at that depth. One of these bodies evidently belonged to Netty Grafton, the ship's stewardess and Alice Bettridge's only female companion during the SS *Kamloops'* final voyage. The other was an unidentified man wearing a wedding ring, whom future divers nicknamed "Grandpa" and "Old Whitey".

A number of divers who have explored the wreck of the SS *Kamloops* following her discovery in 1977 have reported an eerie phenomenon endemic to that underwater graveyard. The body of Old Whitey, they say, moved about the ship throughout the course of their aqueous escapades as if on its own accord. Some divers swear that they were approached by the chalk-white corpse while examining the perfectly-preserved candy wrappers that lay about the wreckage. Others claim to have witnessed the colorless cadaver float towards their hapless diving partners while the latter's attention were diverted. Many of those who have written on the subject have dismissed Old Whitey's alarming antics as the result of underwater currents unconsciously produced by the divers themselves. Others have ascribed the corpse's uncanny animation to the spirit of the sailor who once inhabited it, doomed to wander the decks of the ship whose violent and untimely demise coincided with his own. Whatever the case, the nature of Old Whitey's activity remains one of the many secrets held by the SS *Kamloops*, which sank quickly and mysteriously nearly a century ago.

SS *Bannockburn*: The Flying Dutchman of the Great Lakes

No compilation of the nautical mysteries of Canada's Great Lakes would be complete without a nod to the SS *Bannockburn*, a steamship which disappeared somewhere in Lake Superior on a snowy November day in 1902. To this day, the wreck of the SS *Bannockburn* remains undiscovered despite, some say, the efforts of her ghostly crew, who are said to appear to sailors from time to time on the decks of their phantom vessel, perhaps in the vicinity of their final resting place, before vanishing into thin air.

The SS *Bannockburn* was constructed in 1893 by the British shipbuilding magnate Sir Raylton Dixon. The 245-ton steamer was designed to fit through the Welland Canal and equipped with a steel hull for added protection. She was launched that same year and sent across the Atlantic and up the St. Lawrence to her new home on the Great Lakes.

Throughout the course of her life, the SS *Bannockburn* was plagued by misfortune. In April 1897, she ran into a cluster of sea rocks near the Snake Island Lighthouse on Lake Ontario southwest of Kingston. She began to take on water, forcing her crew to dump much her cargo onto the lake in order to keep her afloat. The ship was subsequently patched up and put back into service, only to suffer another mishap several months later. In October 1897, while hauling a load of grain from Chicago to Kingston, the SS *Bannockburn* hit the wall of the Welland Canal and foundered in that shallow waterway.

The SS *Bannockburn* began what would be her final earthly voyage on November 20th, 1902, leaving Fort William with 85,000 bushels of wheat in her hold. While leaving port, she grounded in shallow water. Although the accident did not appear to damage the ship in any way, it was decided that the voyage would be postponed until the following day.

On November 21st, the SS *Bannockburn* set out once again for Georgian Bay, at the eastern end of Lake Huron, skirting the northern shores of Lake Superior. Her 21-man crew sailed her without incident to a point about 40 miles northeast of Isle Royale, where she was spotted by the captain of another Great Lakes freighter named James McMaugh. Using his binoculars, the captain checked on the ship periodically as he passed her. After attending to some business on his own vessel, McMaugh raised his binoculars once again and discovered, to his surprise, that the *Bannockburn* was nowhere to be seen. Before he could relocate the ship, a heavy fog rolled in and obscured his vision. Captain McMaugh supposed that the mist must have shrouded the *Bannockburn*, concealing it from his view, and continued on his way.

That night, the Witch of November reared her ugly head and swept across Lake Superior, whipping up waves and buffeting boats. At about 11:00 p.m., through a haze of windblown snow, the crew of a passenger steamer called the SS *Huronic* spied a pattern of ship lights which they recognized as the *Bannockburn's*. The freighter did not appear to be in distress, and the two vessels passed each other without incident.

The crew members of the SS *Huronic* were perhaps the last men to set eyes on the SS *Bannockburn*, at least in physical form. When the freighter missed her appointment at Soo Locks, few were overly concerned, assuming that her crew had taken shelter somewhere to wait out the storm. When the Bannockburn failed to show up the following day, it became clear that some mishap had befallen her. When a week and a half had elapsed, the ship was presumed lost with all hands. As the Kingston-based newspaper the *British Whig* put it in their December 2nd, 1902 issue:

"It is generally conceded that the missing steamer is not within earthly hailing distance, that she has found an everlasting berth in the unexplored depths of Lake Superior,

and that the facts of her foundering will never be known. It is asserted by mariners that the Bannockburn's boilers must have exploded, causing her to sink immediately, without giving those aboard a moment in which to seek escape. If this theory is correct, then the big steamer quickly sank beneath the waves of that great lake, carrying down her crew to a quick and sure death. It is sad to know that so many lives were lost, but the sorrow strikes home the deeper when it is known that the greater part of the crew were well known in this city."

The only trace of the steamer to ever surface was a blood-stained life preserver made from cork, which washed up on the shores of Grand Marais, Michigan, at the western end of Lake Superior, on December 15th, 1902. Throughout the winter, divers searched in vain for the wreck of the SS *Bannockburn*. To date, the ship's whereabouts remain unknown.

Legend has it that, every so often, sailors will spot the ghost of *Bannockburn* ploughing her way through the waves of Lake Superior, her lamps flickering and her pilothouse dark, before vanishing into the spray. This legend has become so well-known throughout Wisconsin, Minnesota, and Northern Ontario that the ghost of the *Bannockburn* has acquired the nickname "The *Flying Dutchman* of the Great Lakes", the *Dutchman* being a legendary ghost ship doomed to perpetually sail the turbulent waters off South Africa's Cape of Good Hope. Some say that the crew of the *Bannockburn* willingly endures a similar fate, routinely returning from the Great Beyond to sail the frigid waters of

Lake Superior in the hope that their final resting place will one day be discovered and accorded the respect it deserves.

NOTE FROM THE AUTHOR

Dear Reader,

Thank you for reading *Mysteries of Canada: Volume II*. I hope you enjoyed it as much as I did putting it together. If you're a fan of the book, please consider leaving a review on Amazon.com.

If you have any questions, comments, or concerns about this book, or would simply like to get in touch, please feel free to shoot me an email at:

        Hammerson@HammersonPeters.com.

All the best,

Hammerson Peters

Hammerson Peters

BIBLIOGRAPHY

MYSTERY OF THE SHAKING TENT

- *The Arctic Forests* (1924), by Michael H. Mason

- *Les Voyages du Sieur de Champlain* (1613), by Samuel de Champlain

- *The Jesuit Relations: Volume VI* (1634), by Father Paul le Jeune

- *Travels and Adventures in Canada and the Indian Territories Between the Years 1760 and 1776* (1809), by Alexander Henry the Elder

- *Wanderings of an Artist Among the Indians of North America* (1859), by Paul Kane

- *The Journal of the Bishop of Montreal During a Visit to the Church Missionary Society's North-West America Mission* (1844), by Bishop George J. Mountain

- *Kitchi-gami: Wanderings Around Lake Superior* (1859), by Johann Georg Kohl

- *Blackfoot Magic*, by Sir Cecil Edward Denny† in the September 1944 issue of the magazine *The Beaver*.

- *Shaking the Wigwam*, by A.G. Black in the December 1934 issue of the magazine *The Beaver*

- *The Weird in Canadian Folklore: Exploring the Supernatural* (1955), by R.S. Lambert

- *Blackfoot Shaking Tent* (1969), by Claude E. Shaeffer

- *Spirit Lodge, a North American Shamansitic Séance*, by Ake Hultkrantz

- *Mystery of the Shaking Tents*, by Francis Dickie in the September 1964 issue of the magazine *Real West*

THE OUIJA BOARD OF COBDEN, ONTARIO

- *The Lost Child*, by Violet Bender of Ottawa, Ontario, in the February 1955 issue of the magazine *Fate*; courtesy of Mr. Gary S. Mangiacopra

HARRISON HOT SPRINGS: THE SASQUATCH CAPITAL OF CANADA

- *Hairy Tribe of Wild Men in Vancouver: Survivors of Race, Believed Extinct, Are Reported*, in the June 6, 1934 issue of *The Marshall News Messenger* (Marshall, Texas)

Bibliography

- *Giant Wild Man Scares Residents,* in the March 3, 1934 issue of the *Oakland Tribune* (Oakland, California)

- *Abominable Snowman: Legend Come to Life* (1961), by Ivan T. Sanderson

THE GIANT RIVER SNAKE OF SOUTHEAST ALBERTA

- *How Medicine Hat Was Named,* in *Indian Tales of the Canadian Prairies* (1894), by James F. Sanderson

- *How Seven Persons Creek Was Named,* in *Indian Tales of the Canadian Prairies* (1894), by James F. Sanderson

- *Earl Willows Tells the Story of the Warrior that Ate the Horned Snake* (2009), by Earl Willows

- *Kitchi-gami: Wanderings Around Lake Superior* (1859), by Johann Georg Kohl

GIANT WHITE WOLF SPOTTED IN NORTHERN SASKATCHEWAN

- Private correspondence between Justin Watkins and Hammerson Peters, 2019

TRAVERSPINE GORILLA: A WILDMAN FROM LABRADOR

- *True North: A Journey Into Unexplored Wilderness* (1933), by Elliot Merrick

- *The Camp-Fire*, in the June 1949 issue of the magazine *Adventure*; courtesy of Mr. Gary S. Mangiacopra

- *Snowman's Land*, in the November 1947 issue of the magazine *Adventure*; courtesy of American researcher Gary S. Mangiacopra

- *Canada's Ape-Men of Labrador: Pre-1946 Accounts of Possible Primitive Surviving Hominoid Encounters as Related by the Native Inhabitants of the Labrador Region of the North American Continent*, by Dr. Dwight C. Smith and Gary S. Mangiacopra in the March 2005 issue of the *North American BioFortean Review*

CRAWLER SIGHTING IN THE NORTHWEST TERRITORIES

- Private correspondence between Don Herbert and Hammerson Peters, 2018, 2019

- Private correspondence between Missy Sterling and Hammerson Peters, 2019

- Reddit posts by user MZULFT10989, 2018

Bibliography

- Reddit post by user LilyBirdGK, 2016
- Reddit post by user Bailbondshman, 2017
- Reddit post by user TossO, 2012
- 4Chan post, 2015
- Erik Knudson's 2012 interview for BBC Radio 4

KELLY CHAMANDY: CANADA'S LAST BEAR OIL SALESMAN

- "Reward Offered for Huge Bird of Prey", in the April 17, 1951 issue of the *Boston Daily Globe;* courtesy of Kevin Guhl
- "Famed Ontario Trader Kelly Chamandy Dead", in the March 3, 1966 issue of *The Brandon Sun;* courtesy of Kevin Guhl
- "Kelly Chamandy", in the February 24, 1966 issue of *The Gazette* (Montreal); courtesy of Kevin Guhl
- "Come-back Seen for Bear Grease", in the July 18, 1951 issue of *The Gazette* (Montreal); courtesy of Kevin Guhl
- "Lost Surveyors Rescued from Peril in North: Weak and Foodless Quebec Crew Cries With Joy When Flier Finds Them in Frozen Muskeg Country. Fifteen Men Lived 39 Days on Flesh of 14 Rabbits. Prayed for Help Since Food Ran Out", in the January 3, 1938 issue of *The Ottawa Evening Citizen;* courtesy of Kevin Guhl

Mysteries of Canada: Volume II

- "Make Escape as Storm Wrecks Boats", in the July 11, 1939 issue of *The Ottawa Evening Citizen;* courtesy of Kevin Guhl
- "Mysterious Bird Four Feet High in Timmins Area", in the April 15, 1961 issue of *The Journal* (Ottawa); courtesy of Kevin Guhl
- "Trader Dead", in the February 28, 1966 issue of the *Ottawa Journal;* courtesy of Kevin Guhl
- "Sends Bear Grease to Philip as Hair Restorer", in the March 28, 1955 issue of the *Ottawa Journal;* courtesy of Kevin Guhl
- "Bear Business Bad", in the June 24, 1954 issue of *The Ottawa Journal;* courtesy of Kevin Guhl
- " 100 Reward Offered for Giant Bird of Prey" in the April 17, 1951 issue of The Pittsburgh Press; courtesy of Kevin Guhl
- "Worth 150 Mystery Bird Said Buzzard", in the April 19, 1951 issue of *The Windsor Star;* courtesy of Kevin Guhl
- "Mystery Bird Four Feet Tall, Like Huge Owl", in the April 17, 1951 issue of the *Windsor Daily Star;* courtesy of Kevin Guhl
- "You Can't Beat Kelly's Bear Grease", by Don Delaplante in the April 1, 1953 issue of *Maclean's* magazine
- "Kelly Chamandy: Bald Northerner Trader Sold Bear Grease Hair Restorer", by Don Delaplante
- Private correspondence between Monty Chamandy and Hammerson Peters

Bibliography

GRANGER TAYLOR: THE SPACEMAN OF VANCOUVER ISLAND

- *Spaceman* (2019), by CBC Docs POV
- *The Man Who Went to Space and Disappeared: The Story of Granger Taylor,* by Tyler Hooper in the June 30, 2016 issue of *VICE*
- *The Strange Disappearance of Granger Taylor,* by Rob Morphy in the October 9, 2012 issue of *Mysterious Universe*
- *Night Shift Nurses and Flying Saucer Men,* by Rob Morphy in the September 30, 2011 issue of *Mysterious Universe*

TOM SUKANEN: THE CRAZY FINN OF SASKATCHEWAN

- http://www.sukanenmuseum.ca tomi tomi2.html; Laurence "Moon" Mullin, Eldon Owens, Dick Meacher; Edited by Erin Lough and Paul Johnson
- http://www.sukanenmuseum.ca tomi tomi3.html; Laurence "Moon" Mullin, Eldon Owens, Dick Meacher; Edited by Erin Lough and Paul Johnson
- http://www.sukanenmuseum.ca tomi tomi4.html; Laurence "Moon" Mullin, Eldon Owens, Dick Meacher; Edited by Erin Lough and Paul Johnson
- http://www.canadashistory.ca Magazine Online-Exclusive Articles Dreams-in-the-Dust-The-Story-of-Tom-Sukanen, Rick Book

THE TRAGEDIES OF GILBERT HEDDEN AND WELSFORD PARKER

- *The Oak Island Mystery* (1967), by R.V. Harris
- *The Secret Treasure of Oak Island* (2004), by D'Arcy O'Connor
- *The Curse of Oak Island: The Story of the World's Longest Treasure Hunt* (2018), by Randall Sullivan
- *Captain Kidd and His Skeleton Island* (1935), by Harold T. Wilkins
- "Mystery of the Pirate's Chart" in the December 1950 issue of *FATE*; courtesy of American Fortean researcher Mr. Gary S. Mangiacopra
- "Shipwreck of the Dry Tortuga" (1958), in *Treasure*, by Bill Burrud Productions; courtesy of Mr. Gary S. Mangiacopra
- "On the Treasure Trail of the Wicked Old Pirates," by Harold T. Wilkins in the February 18, 1940 issue of the *San Francisco Examiner*; courtesy of Mr. Gary S. Mangiacopra
- *Maps, Mystery, and Interpretation: 1,2, 3* (2013), by G.J. Bath
- *Treasure and Intrigue: The Legacy of Captain Kidd* (2002), by Graham Harris
- *The Pirate Hunter: The True Story of Captain Kidd* (2002), by Richard Zacks
- *The Campbell Machine,* by Alec Nevala-Lee, in the July/August 2018 issue of *Analog Science*

Bibliography

Fiction/Science Fact; courtesy of Mr. Gary S. Mangiacopra

GHOSTLY TALES OF THE BANFF SPRINGS HOTEL

- http://hammersonpeters.com/?p=964 (2016), by Hammerson Peters

GHOSTLY TALES OF THE PRINCE OF WALES HOTEL

- *Glacier Ghost Stories* (2013), by Karen Stevens
- *A Historical Handbook for the Employees of the Prince of Wales Hotel* (May 2016), by the Glacier Park Foundation
- "Woman Loses Arm in Wreck at Waterton: Cars Collide Near Hotel- Drive Has Three Ribs Broken", in the August 10, 1928 issue of the *Lethbridge Herald*
- "Aging Prince of Wales Buildings Under Inspectors' Scrutiny", in the August 7, 1977 issue of the *Lethbridge Herald*
- "Labour Dept. Probing Waterton Park Hotel", in the August 7, 1977 issue of the *Lethbridge Herald*
- "Hotel Worker Dead Following Waterton Jump," in the September 15, 1977 issue of the *Lethbridge Herald*

CANADA'S LOST WORLDS

The Lands of Viking Legend

- *Saga of Erik the Red* (13th Century), author unknown
- *The Farfarers: Before the Norse* (1988), by Farley Mowat

The Lost Kingdom of Saguenay

- *The Glorious Kingdom of Saguenay*, by Joseph Edward King in the 1950 issue of the *Canadian Historical Review*
- *Jacques Cartier*, by Bernard Allaire in the August 29, 2013 issue of the *Canadian Encyclopedia*

The Isle of Demons

- *Andre Thevet's North America: A Sixteenth-Century View* (1986), by Roger Schlesinger and Arthur P. Stabler
- *Heptameron* (1558), by Queen Marguerite de Navarre
- *Sea Birds, Castaways, and Phantom Islands off Newfoundland*, by J.R. Carpenter in a speech at the British Library on August 7, 2015

The Tropical Valley in the Arctic

- *Legends of the Nahanni Valley* (2018), by Hammerson Peters

Bibliography

TOP 5 CANADIAN CONSPIRACY THEORIES

- The Canadian grapevine
- *The Shag Harbour UFO Incident* (2000), by CBC Maritimes
- *The Valley Without a Head,* in October 2004 issue of *North American BioFortean Review,* by Frank Graves and Ivan T. Sanderson

THE LEGEND OF OLD WIVES LAKE

- http://hammersonpeters.com/?p=1303 (2016), by Hammerson Peters

THE PHENOMENON OF LOST TIME IN CANADA

- Untitled article in the October 1952 issue of the magazine *Fate*; courtesy of Mr. Gary S. Mangiacopra

THE MIRACLE AT LOON LAKE

- *What Saved Mrs. Gowanlock?* by Francis Dickie in the Nov. 1964 issue of *Real West*
- *Two Months in the Camp of Big Bear* (1885), by Theresa Gowanlock and Theresa Delaney
- *Blood Red the Sun* (1926), by William Bleasdell Cameron

- *Capturing Women: The Manipulation of Cultural Imagelry in Canada's Prairie West,* by Sarah Carter
- *The Last Hostage* (1968), by Duncan McLean as told to Eric Wells, "Weekend Magazine No. 32"
- *An Opinion of the Frog Lake Massacre,* by Rev. Dr. Edward Ahenakew in the Summer 1960 issue of the "Alberta Historical Review"
- *An Account of the Frog Lake Massacre,* as told to A.E. Peterson by George Stanley Mesunekwepan), in the Winter 1956 issue of the "Alberta Historical Review"
- *Massacre Street* (September 2010), by Paul William Zits
- *Missions de la Congregation des missionnaires oblats de Marie Immaculee* (December 1885), by Bishop Vital-Justin Grandin

THE PHANTOM TRAIN OF MEDICINE HAT

- *Saamis: The Medicine Hat* (1967), by Senator F.W. Gershaw

NAUTICAL MYSTERIES OF CANADA'S GREAT LAKES

The Wreck of the Edmund Fitzgerald

- *Mighty Fitz: The Sinking of the Edmund Fitzgerald* (2005), by Michael Schumacher

Bibliography

- *Shipwreck: The Mystery of the Edmund Fitzgerald* (1995), by Christopher Rowley and the Discovery Channel

Le Griffon

- *The Discovery of the Great West* (1869), by Francis Parkman
- *The Fighting Governor: A Chronicle of Fronenac* (1915), by Charles William Colby
- *Cavelier de la Salle, Rene-Robert* (1966), by Celine Dupre in the *Dictionary of Canadian Biography: Volume I*
- *The White Whale for Great Lakes Shipwreck Hunters: Inside the Consuming Obsession with Finding the 300-year-old Griffon,* by Sarah Kramer, Bryce Gray, Lizz Giordano, and Anne Arnston in the May 30, 2017 issue of AtlasObscura.com

The *Hamilton* and the *Scourge*

- *Haunted Lakes: Great Lakes Ghost Stories, Superstitions and Sea Serpents* (1997), by Frederick Stonehouse
- *Life Before the Mast* (1843), by James Fennimore Cooper
- *http://www.hamilton-scourge.city.hamilton.on.ca*

Old Whitey and the Ghosts of the SS *Kamloops*

- *The History of the Kamloops,* on SuperiorTrips.com

- *All Hands Lost: Kamloops,* by Curt Bowen in the August 13, 2010 issue of the *Advanced Diver Magazine*
- *Meet Old Whitey, the Preserved Corpse of the SS Kamloops, Lake Superior's Most Haunted Shipwreck,* by Greg Newkirk in the November 27, 2016 issue of WeekInWeird.com

SS *Bannockburn*- The Flying Dutchman of the Great Lakes

- *Likely Lost: No Tidings of the Steamer Bannockburn: Sorrow Here,* in the December 2nd, 1902 issue of the *British Whig*
- *Halloween on the Great Lakes: The Ghost Ship S.S Bannockburn,* on JaysSeaArchaeology.Wordpress.com
- "The Great Lakes Triangle"- Season 3, Episode 8 of *In Search of...* (1978)
- *SS Bannockburn: The Flying Dutchman of the Great Lake,* by Jess Carpenter in the April 2018 issue of GreatLakesBoating.com

An assortment of real Canadian mysteries published on MysteriesOfCanada.com throughout the year 2018. Includes tales of clairvoyance, ghosts, poltergeists, lost treasure, superstitions, haunted hotels, and monsters. Available on Amazon.

Made in the USA
Monee, IL
25 January 2021